A Divided Paradise

CYPRUS 1974-2024

50ᵀᴴ ANNIVERSARY OF TURKISH INTERVENTION

Jim Casey

978-1-915502-89-6 © Jim Casey 2024
@jimcasey4@gmail.com

All rights reserved. No part of this publication may be reproduced, distributed, or transmitted in any form or by any means, including photocopying, recording, or other electronic or mechanical methods, without the prior written permission of the author, except in the case of brief quotations embodied in critical reviews and certain other non-commercial uses. For permission requests, email the author. Published in Ireland by Orla Kelly Publishing.

Orla Kelly Publishing
27 Kilbrody,
Mount Oval,
Rochestown,
Cork,
Ireland

Disclaimer

The information in this book is for general informational purposes only and is not intended as professional advice. The author and publisher make no representations or warranties regarding the accuracy or completeness of the information provided and will not be held liable for any errors or omissions. The opinions expressed in this book are those of the author and do not reflect the official policy or position of any agency or organization.

It is not my intention to favour either side. However, I do express my opinion. I apologise if either sides or persons takes offence to any written text or statements in the book.

In Memoriam

In memory of United Nations Peace-Keeping Force personnel killed while serving the cause of Peace in Cyprus during the Turkish Intervention in 1974.

Guardsman G. Lawson	UK	21/07/1974
Private Lionel Gilbert Perron	Canada	07/07/1974
First Lieutenant Johann Izay	Austria	14/07/1974
Sergeant Paul Decombe	Austria	14/07/1974
Lance-Corporal Ausust Isak	Austria	14/07/1974
Sergeant Benth Schultz Christensen	Denmark	16/07/1974
Private Carsten Busk Anderson	Denmark	16/07/1974
Private Joseph Jean Claude Berger	Canada	10/09/1974
Sergeant Ian Ward Policeman	Australia	14/11/1974

Note: - Private Joseph Jean Claude Berger died on 10th of September 1974 as a result of injuries inflicted on 7th of August 1974.

Sergeant Ian Ward died as a result of a mine explosion in an unmarked minefield previously planted during the conflict.

May they Rest in Peace – Remember Them

DSM Citation Brigadier General Jimmy Flynn DSM (RIP)

He served with the United Nations Peacekeeping Force in Cyprus in 1973-74 as the Liaison Officer to the Greek Cypriot National Guard. He was awarded the Distinguished Service Medal with Distinction for his actions during July and August 1974.

The citation reads: -

"Commandant James J. Flynn while serving with United Nations in Cyprus as Liaison Officer to the Headquarters of the National Guard, during an anti-Government coup and subsequent Turkish intervention in July and August 1974, made an outstanding contribution to the United Nations peacekeeping mission. He displayed to a high degree, the qualities of resourcefulness, initiative, devotion to duty and physical courage in circumstances of grave personal danger and sustained pressure".

An Officer, Gentleman and friend may he Rest in Peace.

The Author - Jim Casey

Jim Casey, born on the 7th of March 1947 in Carley's Bridge, Enniscorthy, Co. Wexford. He joined the Irish Permanent Defence Forces in 1965 and served for 21 years until retirement in 1986. He served in Cyprus on United Nations Missions at HQ UNFICYP in 1967/1968 as Corporal Clerk Operations Branch. 1969/1970 as Corporal Clerk Operations Branch. In 1972 with 22nd Infantry Group Larnaca as Corporal Clerk Operations Section. Again at HQ UNFICYP in 1973/1974 as Sergeant Chief Clerk Operations Branch. In 1977 as Company Sergeant Chief Clerk Operations Branch and in 1984/1985 as Company Sergeant Chief Clerk Humanitarian Branch. He also served with 50th Infantry Battalion in 1982 with UNIFIL in Lebanon as Company Sergeant Headquarter Company.

On retirement from the army in 1986, he took up employment with De Beers Diamonds, a South African Company and served as a diamond courier and security operations for eighteen years until retirement in 2004.

In 2006 he joined Irish United Nations Veterans Association. He held the positions of Chairman Post 30 Galway, Secretary of the Association and then National Chairman. He represented the Association, at his own expense for Saint Patrick's Day parades in 2008 Cabo Roig Spain, 2010 Chicago USA, 2013 Boston USA, 2014 Stockholm Sweden and 2017 Belgium.

In July 2018, Michael Colton Post 1 Dublin and myself as National Chairman, were selected to represent Irish United Nations Veterans Association as part of the Irish delegation to Headquarters, United Nations, New York USA, campaigning for an Irish seat on the Security Council. At HQ United Nations, Michael manned a Congo display stand and I manned a Cyprus display stand. We also attended wreath laying ceremonies and other events during the delegation's visit.

Ireland was successful in securing a seat on the United Nations Security Council. Ireland holds the world record for its commitment to UN Service, since its deployment it has had soldiers serving every single day to present, no other country can make this claim.

HEADQUARTERS UNITED NATIONS NEW YORK

New York Delegation 2018 – UN HQ
Centre Michael Colton and Jim Casey with
Irish Defence Force Personnel

Contents

In Memoriam i
DSM Citation Brigadier General Jimmy Flynn DSM (RIP). ii
The Author - Jim Casey .iii
Introduction 1

Chapter 1 - Introduction to Cyprus 3
Location 3
Area 4
Population 5
Political System 6

Chapter 2 - Brief History of Cyprus 7
Stone Age to Bronze Age 7
Copper 7
From Classical Period to the Romans 9
The Byzantine Empire 10

Chapter 3 - Campaign for Independence and Enosis (Union with Greece) 11
Cyprus Crown Colony 11
EOKA Campaign 12
Cyprus Independence 13

Chapter 4 - Greek and Turkish Cypriot Plus Other Military Involved in 1974 15
   Greek Cypriot National Guard 15
   The Cyprus Naval Command 16
   The Cyprus Air Command 17
   Greek Regiment (ELDYK) and Greek Army 17
   EOKA B 18
   Turkish Cypriot Military 19
   The Turkish Cypriot Fighters 19
   Turkish Regiment (KTKA) 19
   Turkish Army 20

Chapter 5 - Ethnic Conflict 1963 21
   "Bloody Christmas" 1963 and The Green Line 21
   NATO Allies and International Attention 24

Chapter 6 - The Battle of Kokkina 1964 26

Chapter 7 - Deployment United Nations 29
   United Nations Deployment March 1964 29
   Brigadier General Jimmy Flynn DSM (RIP) 29
   Warrant Officers and Sergeants Mess HQ UNFICYP 30

Chapter 8 - Crisis 1967 32

Chapter 9 - Coup d'Etat the 15th July 1974 34
   Coup d'Etat Greek Military Junta Athens Greece 34
   Nicosia International Airport 35
   Nicosia City 36
   News of the Coup D'état Reactions 37

Chapter 10 - The Turkish "Intervention" or "Invasion" 40
   Treaty of Guarantee 40
   Turkish Landings 43
   Greek Cypriot National Guard and ELDYK Regiment Deployment . . 46
   UNFICYP - Full Alert 49

Chapter 11 - The 20th July 1974 50
Kyrenia Area 50
Nicosia City and Nicosia International Airport 55
The Battle for Nicosia International Airport 58
Limassol 63
Paphos 64
Famagusta 65
Village of Alaminos 65

Chapter 12 - The 21st July 1974 67
Nicosia International Airport 68
Kyrenia 71
Nicosia City 72
Lefka 73
Limassol 73
Larnaca 74
Limnitis 75

Chapter 13 - The 22nd July 1974 76
Kyrenia Area 76
Famagusta 77
Nicosia 78

Chapter 14 - The 23rd July 1974 79
Nicosia 79
Kyrenia 82

Chapter 15 - My Involvement In Nicosia International Airport . . 83
Operations Brief the 23rd of July 1974 83
Personal Weapon 84
Drop-off at Nicosia International Airport 84
Situation on Arrival 84
Journalists at Nicosia International Airport 86
Greek Cypriot National Guard plus ELDYK and Turkish Forces . . 87
Order Restored 87

Chapter 16 - The 24th July to 14th August 89
Reinforcements Nicosia International Airport 89
Incidents during the period 89

Chapter 17 - The 14th August Renewal of Turkish Offensive 95
Attila II 95
The Battle of Agios Dometios Nicosia. 98
The 14th of August Greek Cypriot National Guard Eastern Sector
Defences 100
The 14th of August - Famagusta 101
The 14th of August - Villages of Maratha, Santalaris and Aloda . . . 105
The 14th of August - The Villages of Tochni and Zyggi 105
The 15th of August - Tank Battle 106
The 15th of August Greek Cypriot National Guard Defence Lines. . 107
The 15th – 16th of August - Villages of Murataga, Sandallar and Atlilar 108
The 16th of August Greek Cypriot National Guard Sectors. 108
The 16th of August - Prastio Famagusta 109
The 16th and 17th of August - Pyroi and Louroujina 109
The 17th of August - Asha and Sinta 111
The 18th of August - Eptakomi 111
The 18th of August – Angolemi 111
The 19th of August - Nicosia 111
End of Conflict 112

Chapter 18 - Casualties 114
United Nations Casualties 114
Greek Cypriot National Guard Casualties 114
Greek Regiment (ELDYK) and Greek Army Casualties 114
Turkish Cypriot Fighters Casualties 114
Turkish Forces 115
Civilian Casualties 115

Chapter 19 - Evacuations 116

Chapter 20 - Missing Persons 118

Chapter 21 - Refugees. 120

Chapter 22 - Northern Cyprus 122

Chapter 23 - European Commission on Human Rights 124

Chapter 24 - Injustice to Greek Soldiers (ELDYK) Ongoing . . . 126
Injustice 126
The Lawsuit 127
The Appeal 128
The absurdity 128

Chapter 25 - Economic Effects of Partition 129
Republic of Cyprus 129
Turkish Republic of Northern Cyprus. 131

Chapter 26 - Conclusion 133

Abbreviations 137

Acknowledgements 138

Supplementary 139
Ireland and United Nations 139
Roll of Honour. 140
Irish Defence Forces. 144
Irish Veteran Associations 146
Other Veteran Associations 149

General 150
The 1960's. 150

Introduction

"A Divided Paradise" delves into the tumultuous history of Cyprus, its military forces and with the main focus on the events that transpired during 1974, the Coup d'état and Turkish Intervention. It gives a brief introduction to the location/area of Cyprus, history, population and political system. It takes readers on a journey through the catastrophic battles and atrocities between the Turkish and Greek Cypriot communities. This book aims to shed light on the complexities and motivations behind the conflict, while examining the profound human suffering, after effects it had on the island and its people from both communities.

The battles in Cyprus during 1974 resulted in a significant loss of life and injuries on both sides. Soldiers, innocent civilians, and individuals caught in the crossfire paid the ultimate sacrifice. The human cost of the conflict is immeasurable, leaving a profound void in the families and communities of both sides affected by the event.

We should remember the fallen, it is essential to honour their sacrifices by working towards lasting peace. Their memory should be a catalyst for renewed efforts in achieving reconciliation, justice, and a unified Cyprus. Ultimately, it is through peace that we can best honour those who gave their lives in the pursuit of a better future.

This book is compiled from extracts in United Nations operations daily log sheets, situation reports during the Coup d'état and Intervention by Turkish Forces on the 20th of July 1974. Discussions with Commandant James Flynn (RIP) of his experiences and ordeals, on his return to HQ UNFICYP from Greek Cypriot National Guard Headquarters. Also from memory, personal notes, extracts from United Nations humanitarian documents from 1974 to 1977 and personal experience. The dates and times listed may not be the exact date and time the incidents occurred, it may be the date and times reported by the United Nations Sectors to HQ UNFICYP. As with every war, stories and claims abound on both sides. Some of them are almost certainly true, but some are hard to verify.

The war in Cyprus 1974 has become a "forgotten war", except to its victims and families who are still affected after fifty years on. The reasons for this are, the battles in Cyprus are poorly documented, such published records as there are tend to be either in Greek or Turkish. Second, neither Greek Cypriot nor Turkish war logs are available to public scrutiny.

Lastly, Turkey's obsessive culture of military secrecy keeps even historic records locked away indefinitely.

*William Gilbert (left) and Jim Casey (right) guests at State Dinner offered by President of Ireland Michael D Higgins and Sabina Higgins in honour of H.E. Nicos Anastasiades President of the Republic of Cyprus and Andri Anastasiades on the occasion of their State visit to Ireland.
Arus an Uachtarain 18th October 2016.*

Chapter 1
Introduction to Cyprus

National Flag Republic of Cyprus

Location

Cyprus is an island located in the eastern Mediterranean Sea. It is geographically in western Asia. Its cultural ties and geopolitics are overwhelmingly south-eastern European. Cyprus is the third-largest and third-most populous island in the Mediterranean. It is located north of Egypt, east of Greece, south of Turkey, west of Lebanon and Syria.

Cyprus comprises tall mountains, fertile valleys, and wide beaches. The general pattern of its roughly 400-mile (640-km) coastline is indented and rocky, with long, sandy beaches. Troodos is the largest mountain range in Cyprus, located in roughly the centre of the island. Its highest peak is Mount Olympus at 1,952 metres (6,404 feet) The range stretches across most of the western side of Cyprus. The Kyrenia mountains the western portion of which is also known as the Pentadaktylos for its five-fingered shaped peaks extend for 100 miles (160 km) parallel to and just inland from the northern coast. Its highest peak is Mount Selvili, at 1,024m (3,360 feet).

Settled for more than ten millennia, Cyprus stands at a cultural, linguistic, and historic crossroads between Europe and Asia. Its capital and largest city is Nicosia. Since the Turkish intervention of 1974, the northern portion of the island is *de facto* governed by the self-declared "illegal" Turkish Republic of Northern Cyprus in 1983.

Area

The third largest island in the Mediterranean it has a land area of 9,251km². 5,896km² (2,276 square miles) are under the control of the Republic of Cyprus; 3,355km² (1,295 square miles) are de facto under the administration of the self-declared "illegal" Turkish Republic of Northern Cyprus since 1974.

The Island is divided into six districts – Nicosia, Limassol, Paphos, Larnaca, in the north Kyrenia and Famagusta. In addition, two British sovereign bases areas are operational on the Island Akrotiri and Dhekelia.

Population

Cyprus has a population of approximately 1.2 million people living on the island. Since 1974/1975 in the region of 875,900 Greek Cypriot people live in the Republic of Cyprus and 326,000 Turkish Cypriots and Turkish Nationalists live in the Turkish Republic of Northern Cyprus, Turkish Nationals greatly outnumber the Turkish Cypriots. The figure in Northern Cyprus is believed to be much greater, in the region of 500,000 Turkish Cypriot and Turkish Nationals.

In 1960 when Independence was granted by the United Kingdom, the approximate distribution of the population of Cyprus was 77.1% Greek Cypriot, 18.2% Turkish Cypriot, 4.7% other communities, primarily Armenians and Maronites dispersed throughout the entire island. These figures do not include British military and civilians based in the Sovereign Based Areas.

In 1963 after the ethnic conflict between Greek and Turkish Cypriots, the Turkish majority withdrew into enclaves resulting in a change of population distribution statics.

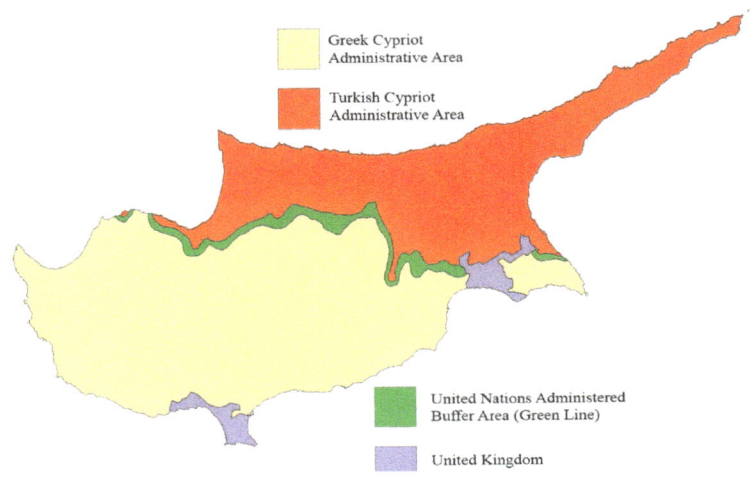

Political System

Cyprus is a presidential republic

The president is both head of state and government. Despite joining the European Union on the 1st of May 2004, as a de facto divided island, the whole island of Cyprus is European Union territory. Turkish Cypriots who have, or are eligible for, European Union travel documents are European Union citizens. European Union law is suspended in areas where the Cypriot government (Government of the Republic) does not exercise effective control. Cyprus has two official languages: Greek and Turkish, only Greek is the official European Union language. I am of the opinion, if Greek is the official language according to the European Union, it is discrimination against the Turkish Cypriots, who have European Union rights. They should be able to complete all documents in their native language and it should be recognised by the European Union.

Chapter 2
Brief History of Cyprus

Stone Age to Bronze Age

The Island of Cyprus was originally occupied by an ancient civilisation during the Stone Age. During this period, it is envisaged that this population brought about the extinction of many species of animal, including the pygmy hippopotamus and the dwarf elephant. There have been many discoveries that have led archaeologists to understand these ancient peoples. For example, the discovery of a water well in western Cyprus is believed to be among the oldest in the world, and is thought to show the sophistication of these early settlers and their ability to live in harmony with their environment. There is also some evidence of settlements that date from this period with artefacts showing contact with other civilisations beyond the island of Cyprus, with imports from Anatolia, which can be found in modern Turkey.

Copper

The use of copper began at around the 4th millennium BC, marking the dawn of the Bronze Age. The mines were operational for centuries until other mineral sources were discovered, in other areas, thus the mines remained neglected for centuries until they were reopened shortly before *World War I*. They were subsequently exploited from 1925 until they were closed during the *Great Depression* of the 1930s Production resumed after *World War II*, and copper and other minerals were exported. The island's most important copper mines are located in the area of Skouriotissa in the Turkish-occupied zone, but copper ore reserves declined substantially.

During this time copper replaced stone and trade with Egypt and many Aegean islands were established alongside importation from Greece. There is evidence of the advanced nature of the society living during the Bronze Age in Cyprus and rather than an ancient and unsophisticated people there is a great deal of evidence of the advanced nature of the society including jewellery, pottery and ivory carvings. Most importantly this period in history saw the development of a linear script writing called Cypro-Minoa.

These copper mines were in use during the middle sixties up to the late seventies.

United Nations Irish soldiers served in the Lefka District, beside the copper mines in 1966 up to the 1970's, under canvas tents.

Copper Mine Skouriotissa

An Irish soldier on duty in one of the substandard sentry boxes "sweat box" in Lefka District 1969.

From Classical Period to the Romans

Roman Ruins Salamis west of Famagusta

The classical period in Cyprus spanned a similar timeframe as that of mainland Greece dating between 475-325BC. This was an era that gave witness to a large improvement in the economics of Cyprus and underwent a lot of political changes including episodes of rule by the Assyrians, Egyptians and Persians. Although Cyprus maintained strong links to Greece. The last Persian ruler was overthrown by Alexander the Great, who in turn was overthrown by Ptolemy of Egypt. Cyprus remained under Egyptian control for over 250 years until it was annexed to the Roman Empire in 58BC where it remained for approximately 600 years.

The Byzantine Empire

After the division of the Roman Empire, Cyprus found itself under Byzantine rule until the 650's AD when the island was invaded by the Arabs. This resulted in a joint Arab and Byzantine rule. Under their rule, Christianity flourished, and numerous magnificent churches and monasteries were built.

In the 12th century AD The Crusaders arrived, led by Richard the Lionheart of England, who took control from the Byzantines.

Eventually, the British sold the island to the Knights Templar leading to a huge level of Templar history and mythology located in Cyprus. The Templars in turn sold Cyprus to the King of Jerusalem, which led to the national language becoming French. From 1489 Cyprus found itself under Venetian rule, but this was taken by the Ottomans in 1570. The Ottoman rule lasted for approximately 300 years.

During this period, the island witnessed significant changes in its demographics and religious composition. The Ottoman administration introduced a system known as the Millet system, which recognized separate legal status for each religious community, including the Greek Orthodox, Maronite, Armenian, and Jewish communities.

Chapter 3
Campaign for Independence and Enosis (Union with Greece)

Cyprus Crown Colony

After the Cyprus Convention in 1878 the government of Cyprus was turned into a United Kingdom protectorate. It was then made a Crown Colony in 1925. During this period the idea of Greek Cypriot nationalism began to take root among the Greek Cypriot population. It fuelled aspirations for enosis, or the unification of Cyprus with Greece.

Alongside Greek Cypriot nationalism, a Turkish Cypriot identity also developed during this period. Turkish Cypriots, who had gradually become a minority population on the island, sought to preserve their cultural and political rights as a distinct identity. In the early 1950s, a Greek nationalist group was formed called (EOKA) or "National Organisation of Cypriot Fighters". Their objective was to drive the British out of the island first, gain their independence and then to integrate the island with Greece (Enosis). EOKA wished to remove all obstacles from their path to independence and union with Greece (Enosis).

The British ruled the Island until 1960, during their rule they had implemented administrative and social reforms, modernizing the infrastructure and educational system.

EOKA Campaign

In 1955 the campaign for Enosis was led by Archbishop Makarios of the Cyprus Orthodox Church and Colonel George Grivas, head of National Organisation of Cypriot Fighters (EOKA). They aimed to achieve independence and Enosis by attacking government, military installations and by mobilising the civilian population to demonstrate against the British Forces presence. EOKA militants launched an armed insurgency against British colonial rule, demanding Enosis, the union of Cyprus with Greece. They were aided and assisted by the National Front of Cyprus (EMAK), which provided EOKA with intelligence, supplies, weapons, medicines, recruits and safe houses. The Turkish Cypriots, fearing marginalization within a Greek-dominated state, resisted Enosis and favoured the idea of Taksim or partition.

From the 1st until the end of April 1955 EOKA commenced a series of bombing attacks on government offices in Nicosia the capital city and other locations, a total of eighteen bomb attacks occurred. From the 19th until the end June 1955 they then began a campaign of assassinations mainly aimed at the Greek Cypriot police force and any Greek Cypriots who disagreed with the idea of Enosis. It organised rioting by students and schoolchildren. It used execution squads to target the police, military personnel and their families. EOKA kept up the pressure on Britain by extending their campaign to the towns of Cyprus, where they attacked British servicemen and their families. Since the beginning of the campaign, a total of two hundred and four bombings and attacks occurred. These attacks continued throughout 1955 to 1958, until the London Zurich Agreements and President Makarios had abandoned his initial demand for Enosis.

It is estimated the EOKA campaign resulted in the death of three hundred and seventy-one British soldiers, thirty-nine Turkish Cypriot Policemen, fifteen Greek Cypriot Policemen. Civilians – two hundred and three Greek

Cypriots, twenty-two Turkish Cypriots and twenty-six British. A total of one hundred and twelve EOKA were killed, this includes nine executed.

Cyprus Independence

On the 16th of August 1960, Cyprus was reborn as The Independent Republic of Cyprus. This day of Independence is celebrated every year with a public holiday in Cyprus.

When independence was gained from the British, the United Kingdom held 2% of the island, which are military bases with a number of other locations in use on the island, namely Akrotiri, Episkipi, Dhekelia, RAF Nicosia, a monitoring station on Mount Olympus in the Troodos mountains, and various antenna arrays in Ayios Nikolaos, near Famagusta. Via varied formal agreements and informal arrangements, the United States enjoys some access to and benefits from these United Kingdom facilities.

The Provisions of the Constitution of Cyprus: - "The Greek and Turkish Cypriot communities of Cyprus opposed to each other: - thirty-five seats in the parliament belonged to the Greek Cypriots and fifteen to the Turkish Cypriots. The Government consists of seven ministerial portfolios to the Greek Cypriots and three to the Turkish Cypriots. The President could only be Greek Cypriot and the Vice President Turkish Cypriot".

Archbishop Makarios emerged as a prominent Greek Cypriot leader, winning the Presidency. Fazıl Küçük was the elected Turkish Cypriot Vice President. The formal equality of rights meant infringement on the rights of the Turkish Cypriots, who were not resigned to this situation.

Despite a power-sharing arrangement between Greek and Turkish Cypriots, tensions persisted, leading to intermittent outbreaks of intercommunal violence in the years following.

President Makarios's complicated relationship with both Greek and Turkish Cypriot communities. His attempts to maintain a delicate balance between nationalist aspirations and calls for unity often left both sides feeling frustrated and marginalized. Makarios was seen as favouring Greek Cypriots, which galvanized support for Turkish Cypriot separatism.

Vice President Fazil Kucuk and Archbishop Makarios

The economic conditions on the island also played a significant role in the unravelling of Cyprus. Rising unemployment, inflation, and economic disparities fuelled social discontent. Greek Cypriot dominance in the business and agricultural sectors further deepened the divide between the two communities.

Chapter 4

Greek and Turkish Cypriot Plus Other Military Involved in 1974

Greek Cypriot National Guard

The Greek Cypriot National Guard were established in 1964 after the intercommunal violence known as "Bloody Christmas" *(Chapter 5)*. Its nominal total wartime strength was forty thousand soldiers, of whom about thirty thousand were to be mobilised reservists.

It was equipped with surplus equipment from Greece, mainly of British origin. A total of forty Marmon Herrington Mk-IVF armoured vehicles armed with QF-2 pounder 40mm anti-tank guns. It was reinforced by a purchase of Soviet weapons in 1965. It included thirty-two T-34 medium Russian made tanks with 85mm guns. Eighty six field artillery pieces consisting of fifty four 25-pounder field guns 87.6mm calibre, twenty M-1944 field guns 100mm calibre, four 3.7 AA guns 94mm calibre and eight M-116 pack howitzers 75mm calibre. It had about one hundred BTR-152 Russian armoured vehicles with Gorvunov 7.62mm co-axial machine guns and various personal weapons. The Greek Cypriot National Guard were controlled by officers from Greece, strength of about one thousand plus, so technically they were controlled by the Greek Military Junta in Athens.

In 1972 President Makarios founded the Greek Cypriot Tactical Reserve Corps ("Efedrikon Soma"). It was a large police force to reinforce the National Guard in wartime, in fact however, it was Makarios' trusted counterweight against the Athens-controlled Greek Cypriot National Guard. This force was much like EOKA B an equally potent "force for evil". It was lightly equipped with modern Czechoslovakian-supplied weapons and well trained in military style tactics. It comprised 3 battalions.

In 1972 President Makarios acquired four medium tanks for use by this force. They were secretly stored along with other weapons and ammunition in a warehouse at Nicosia International Airport. This warehouse was immediately impounded and taken over by United Nations Forces on the 16th of July 1974, to prevent them being used at the start of the coup d'état by Greek Cypriot Forces.

During the Turkish intervention the Greek Cypriot National Guard, was for the first time in its history faced with a supreme task, to defend the independence and territorial integrity of the Republic of Cyprus. In conditions of division, they put up strong resistance and fought fierce battles, with no naval, air support and old weapons, they inflicted significant deaths, losses and shooting down a number of aircraft of a well-equipped modern NATO trained army.

The Cyprus Naval Command

The Cyprus Naval Command also known as the Cyprus Navy or Cypriot Navy, founded in 1964, is the armed sea wing of the Cypriot National Guard. The Cyprus Naval Command has the primary mission of defending the maritime borders of the Republic of Cyprus. This force does not possess any capital ships or other major warships, but is equipped with patrol boats, landing craft, surface-to-surface missile systems and integrated radar systems, as well as SEALs-type naval underwater demolitions units. Its strength is usually four hundred and sixty personnel. During the Turkish intervention the Cyprus Naval Command played no major part, with the exception of sending two torpedo boats the T-1 and T-3 to intersect the Turkish Navy approaching Cyprus which led to their destruction.

The Cyprus Air Command

The Cyprus Air Command also known as the Cyprus Air Force or Cypriot Air Force, founded on the 16th of August 1960. It is the armed air wing of the National Guard. This force is equipped with light aircraft, attack and anti-tank helicopters, surface-to-air missile systems and integrated radar systems. It had a strength of one thousand two hundred personnel.

It mainly performs search and rescue tasks (SAR), transport of the sick, control of fires, marine pollution as well as defence and police force operations on the Cypriot coast and territory.

The Cyprus Air Command played no role during the Turkish intervention. It is mainly geared for civilian duties.

Greek Regiment (ELDYK) and Greek Army

A Greek Regiment was also deployed in Cyprus (ELDYK). It was authorised under the Treaty of Alliance in August 1960. It was not under the National Guard's direct control. It consisted of two infantry battalions, with one thousand two hundred soldiers (nominal nine hundred and fifty). It was well trained and organized but equipped with light and old weapons. ELDYK's units were dispatched to various places in order to help the Greek Cypriot National Guard. Along with ELDYK, Greece managed to involve an airborne battalion of two hundred troops landing in Nicosia International Airport and four hundred and fifty troops landing at Paphos.

During the Turkish intervention, the Greek Regiment (ELDYK) fought bravely against the Turkish Forces in several battles their units were dispatched to various places in Cyprus in order to help the Greek Cypriot National Guard.

EOKA B

Another paramilitary force was EOKA B (Greek Cypriot Paramilitary Association), originally EOKA (National Organisation of Cypriot Fighters) formed in 1955, by General George Grivas. They were dispended in 1978. They were anti-colonialist freedom fighters, fighting for independence from Great Britain. In 1971 Grivas renamed it EOKA B in support of the Military Junta in Athens Greece. It had about five thousand members with approximately one thousand firearms. They were involved in organising the coup d'état with Greek Cypriot National Guard and the Military Junta in Athens.

During the intervention, the ordinary Greek Cypriots and Greek Cypriot soldiers were desperately defending themselves against the Turkish Forces, most of EOKA B carried out ethnic cleansing operations in the rear against dissident democrats and Turkish Cypriots.

Smaller paramilitaries also existed, under political leaders and their lieutenants, numbers unknown.

Turkish Cypriot Military

The Turkish Cypriot Fighters

The Turkish Cypriot Resistance Organisation (TMT) was founded by Rauf Denktaş and Turkish military officer Rıza Vuruşkan in1958, as an organisation to counter the Greek Cypriot Fighter's Organization EOKA. It later was referred to Turkish Cypriot Fighters. The total strength of the Turkish-Cypriot Fighters was, twenty seven infantry battalions, grouped into eight regiments, and a strength of potentially up to twenty thousand fighters. The Turkish-Cypriot Battalions were lightly armed with light semi-automatic infantry weapons and M1 carbines. With absolutely no support from artillery, tanks, nor any other mechanized means to assist them wage warfare. They were under strength and were generally limited to defensive capabilities. They also trained for unconventional operations, such as sabotage, ambushes etc. They were deployed in the Turkish Cypriot Enclaves throughout the island. They assisted the Turkish Forces during the intervention.

Turkish Regiment (KTKA)

A Turkish Regiment was also deployed in Cyprus (KTKA), with a strength of nine hundred and fifty men (nominal six hundred and fifty), organised in two divisions, within the Turkish Cypriot Enclaves of Asha Paşaköy the 28th Infantry Division Headquarters to the northeast of Nicosia and at Camlibel within the district of Kyrenia the 39th Infantry Division Headquarters. It was equipped with M 47 tanks, artillery, APCs M-113 and other weaponry. It was also authorised under the Treaty of Alliance August 1960. They assisted the Turkish Forces during the intervention.

Turkish Army

The main intervention force on the 20th of July 1974, was in the region of three thousand troops and further landings were in the region of thirty-seven thousand troops. These were Parachute Brigade, Commando Brigade, Special Strike Force Landing Brigade, two Infantry Divisions, Navy and an Armoured Brigade. They were equipped with M-47 and M-48 tanks, armoured fighting vehicles, M-113 armoured personnel carriers, self-propelled howitzers, multiple rocket launchers, anti-tank missiles, artillery, recoilless rifles M-40A1, mortars various calibres and personal weapons. They were also supported by the Turkish air force and navy.

On the 21st of July 1974 the Turkish Forces had captured 3% of the island before a ceasefire was declared. Turkish Forces enlarged their original beachhead in August 1974 resulting in the capture and occupation of approximately 36% of the island.

Chapter 5
Ethnic Conflict 1963

"Bloody Christmas" 1963 and The Green Line

In 1963 ethnic conflict raged in Cyprus as a constitutional battle pitted the island's majority Greek Cypriots against the less numerous Turkish Cypriots. The spark that ignited the conflict of violence happened at 02.30 hours on the 21st of December 1963 when Greek Cypriot 'special constables' shot dead two Turkish Cypriots who refused to show their identity cards. The incident happened near the Turkish Market in Nicosia.

The funeral of the two Turkish Cypriots took place at 15.00 hours on Sunday the 22nd of December 1963, an event where calm prevailed, but later that night shootings began in many parts of Nicosia, in other towns and villages across the island. Shooting incidents were reported in over one hundred villages that night. The fighting continued throughout Monday, the 23rd and Tuesday 24th of December and was especially fierce along the line of the Pedieos river in Nicosia very close to the British High Commission. Greek Cypriot National Guard, police and armed irregulars, mostly EOKA, launched a massive attack on the Turkish Cypriot enclaves in Nicosia, towns and villages. They captured the Turkish Cypriot enclaves and the irregulars ran wild, killing scores of Turkish Cypriots, including women and children, smashing and looting homes and taking hundreds of hostages.

Also, the situation was fuelled by President Makarios attempting to modify the Constitution. The leading cause of disagreements was the ratio of Greek Cypriots to Turkish Cypriots in the civil service. Turkish Cypriots complained that the seventy-to-thirty ratio was not enforced. Greek Cypriots felt that the provisions discriminated against them, because they constituted almost eighty percent of the population. Another major point of contention concerned the composition of units under the sixty-to- forty ratio decreed for the Greek Cypriot National Guard Army. President Makarios favoured complete integration.

Greek Cypriot National Guard initiated a military campaign against the Turkish Cypriots and began to attack Turkish Cypriot villages, one hundred and three villages were destroyed. On the 23rd of December, a ceasefire was agreed upon by President Makarios and Turkish Cypriot leadership. However, fighting continued and intensified in Nicosia and Larnaca. Machine guns were fired from mosques in Turkish Cypriot inhabited areas. The main victims of the numerous incidents that took place during the next few months were Turkish Cypriots. Seven hundred Turkish Cypriot hostages were taken, including women and children, from the northern suburbs of Nicosia. On the 23rd of December 1964 Nikos Sampson led a group of Greek Cypriot irregulars into the mixed suburb of Omorphita and massacred the Turkish Cypriot population indiscriminately. After this, the centre of the capital was dubbed "Murder Mile". By 1964, one hundred and ninety-three Turkish Cypriots and one hundred and thirty-three Greek Cypriots were killed, with a further two hundred and nine Turkish Cypriots and forty-one Greek Cypriot missing, presumed dead. By early 1964, the Turkish Cypriots started to withdraw into enclaves where the Greek Cypriots then blockaded them, resulting in some twenty five thousand Turkish Cypriots becoming refugees, or internally "displaced persons" from one hundred and three villages. Around five hundred Greek Cypriots and one thousand two hundred Armenians were also displaced. This was known as "Bloody Christmas" with one hundred and seventy-four Greek Cypriots and three hundred and sixty-four Turkish Cypriots killed in the conflict.

The events of "Bloody Christmas" abruptly brought about the end of the power-sharing arrangement in the government of Cyprus, leaving the police and civil service to become de facto Greek Cypriot organisations. This was mainly because Turkish Cypriots felt too unsafe to leave their local enclaves and go to work in Greek Cypriot-majority places, particularly because of revenge murders caused by the anti-Turkish Cypriot broadcasts on Greek-language radio. This also prompted Greek Cypriot employers to lay off their Turkish Cypriot employees, while some Turkish Cypriots resigned their positions of their own volition. As a result, United Nations troops were deployed (Chapter 7) establishing the United Nations Buffer Zone (commonly called the Green Line) was marked out in 1964 as a temporary measure to restore peace after a decade of inter-communal fighting between Greek and Turkish Cypriots.

Irish UN Troops evacuating Turkish Cypriots 1964.

Following this intercommunal violence and establishment of the Green Line, a relatively stable situation ensued on the island. With the Turkish-Cypriot population now living in enclaves, each comprising several villages, and having its own Turkish Cypriot Armed Fighters.

The biggest Turkish-Cypriot enclave was the (1) Nicosia– St. Hilarion enclave, also called Günyeli enclave. With a twenty-five thousand strong populations, out of a total of one hundred and seventeen thousand Turkish-Cypriots on the island. It included the northern district of Nicosia and spanned north to the Pentadaktylos mountain range, but had no access to the sea.

In 1964 Turkish-Cypriot Fighters occupied the Bogaz pass without a fight. Greek-Cypriot National Guard efforts to dislodge them by force were unsuccessful. As a result, the Turkish-Cypriot Fighters had control of the Nicosia to Kyrenia main road, and access to the coastal area north of the Pentadaktylos mountains. With the Bogaz pass in Turkish hands, the Greek Cypriot National Guard and civilians had to use longer routes to access the north coast, namely via the Panagra pass, on western Pentadaktylos mountains. UNFICYP soldiers provided escorts to Greek Cypriot civilians on the main Nicosia to Kyrenia road to ensure their safe passage through the Turkish Cypriot areas.

Significant Turkish-Cypriot enclaves were: -

1. Nicosia
2. Famagusta
3. Lefka
4. Tziaos (Serdarli)
5. Limassol
6. Larnaca
7. Paphos
8. Limnitis
9. Kokkina
10. Louroujina.

NATO Allies and International Attention

The situation would have generated very little international attention except that the Greek and Turkish Cypriot communities on the island were supported by Greece and Turkey, both of whom were NATO allies.

Concern grew, within the NATO membership, for the security of the alliance. The countries involved in the conflict, known collectively as NATO's southern flank, extended NATO's intelligence and missile range due to their close proximity to the Soviet Union. The British sovereign bases in Cyprus also offered a significant strategic advantage to NATO since its airfields supported U2 spy aircraft and nuclear-equipment.

Chapter 6
The Battle of Kokkina 1964

In mid-1964, the Greek Cypriot Government surmised that the Turkish Cypriots, who had universally receded into enclaves, were becoming increasingly well equipped with small arms, squad automatic weapons and mortars that would not have been made available to them through legal ports of entry.

The Turkish Cypriots held a deep-water dock at Kokkina, in Tillyria region, this area was suspected as the focus of a Turkish shipping point for the illegal import of arms to the Turkish Cypriot Fighters from mainland Turkey.

View of Kokkina Turkish Cypriot Enclave

On the 6th of August 1964, the Greek Cypriot National Guard commenced an attack on the Turkish enclave of Kokkina for two days, Greek Cypriot National Guard laid down support fire with six 25-pounder guns and approximately twelve mortars, coordinated with 20mm and 40mm cannon fire from the Cyprus Naval boats *Phaethon* and *Arion*. Under this barrage, the Greek Cypriot National Guard progressed slowly into the enclave with cover from overlapping machine gun fire, but found that the Turkish Cypriot Fighters had organised their own machine guns and mortars into an effective formation. The battle quickly degraded into a low-intensity exchange of sniping and support fire, as both sides dug into the difficult terrain. The United Nations troops were withdrawn from the area during the battle.

On the morning of the 8th of August 1964, the Cypriot patrol boats *Phaethon* and *Arion* were attacked by Turkish Air Force jets as they sailed close to Xeros Harbour in Morphou Bay. The boats commenced evasive manoeuvres and put up anti-aircraft fire. The *Phaethon* was quickly strafed with 75mm rockets and burst into flames, killing seven crew members and wounding an unknown number of the crew. It's engine still running, the surviving crew managed to guide it aground and then abandoned ship. As the *Arion* continued to evade the attack, a second formation of Turkish F-100 Super Sabre jets came in low to attack it. One of the jets was shot down by the Greek Cypriot National Guard defence. The *Arion* was reportedly struck several times, but managed to escape to Paphos. Between the 8th and 9th of August 1964, the Turkish Air Force was given free rein to attack multiple targets in the Kokkina area, including a number of Greek Cypriot villages. Such heavy bombing caused significant casualties among the civilian population. Greek Cypriot civilian casualties were reported as a result of heavy air attacks against several populated locations, including Kato Pyrgos by the dropping of incendiary napalm bombs. Turkish jets also attacked sites occupied by the Greek Cypriot National Guard, killing a number of military personnel and destroying a Marmon Herrington Mk-IVF armoured car.

The immediate geographical result of the conflict in the Kokkina area was, the evacuation of four villages. The Kokkina enclave was effectively reduced to a narrow beachhead. The Greek Cypriot National Guard had failed to storm the inner defences of the enclave, thus leaving the Turkish Cypriot beachhead essentially intact.

The threat of a Turkish military escalation and a resolution of the United Nations Security Council calling for a ceasefire, ended the stand-off. A ceasefire was declared on the 9th of August 1964 and UNFICYP forces were once again deployed to the area. Fighting in the region ceased on the 10th of August 1964, but Kokkina's value to the Turkish military dwindled, as the Greek Cypriots had effectively isolated it from the coastal road.

Chapter 7
Deployment United Nations

United Nations Deployment March 1964

With instability jeopardizing the entire southern flank of its area of operation, the Cyprus crisis shook NATO's ability to detect and respond to potential threats. As a result, negotiations by both sides and United Nations HQ New York, agreed that Britain, Canada, Ireland and Sweden would make up a United Nations force. On the 13th of March, 1964, United Nations Secretary-General U Thant announced that a United Nations force would be established consisting of these nations, along with possible commitments from Finland and Austria, which they later committed to. Ireland served in its role until October 1973 when the contingent was withdrawn in support of the United Nations Emergency Force during the Yom Kippur War. However, Ireland continued to deploy a small staff to HQ UNFICYP.

In 1974 three Irish soldiers served at HQ UNFICYP beside Nicosia International Airport. They were Comdt. James Flynn – Liaison Officer to Cypriot National Guard Army, CQMS Tony Byrne – Chief Clerk Humanitarian Branch and I, Sergeant Jim Casey – Chief Clerk Operations Branch. We were the only Irish soldiers serving on the island.

Brigadier General Jimmy Flynn DSM (RIP)

In July 1974, the world was transfixed by the Watergate Scandal which threatened to topple the Presidency of Richard Nixon. Events in Cyprus threatened the stability of the NATO alliance at the height of the Cold War. The sudden intervention of Cyprus by Turkey left NATO allies scrambling to calm the situation.

It was at that moment that the United Nations Force in Cyprus (UNFICYP), the peacekeepers were put directly in the line of fire as they protected civilians and deprived critical infrastructure from the belligerents. The year 1974 marked the tenth anniversary of the United Nations Force in Cyprus (UNFICYP). After ten years of relative calm, United Nations peacekeepers could be forgiven for not understanding what Cyprus was like when their first comrades played a significant part in Cyprus during its constitutional crisis of 1963-1964.

The United Nations Forces in Cyprus (UNFICYP) played a critical role in addressing the Cyprus issue and promoting peacekeeping efforts. They monitored the ceasefire and maintained a buffer zone, known as the Green Line, between the Greek Cypriot and Turkish Cypriot communities.

Warrant Officers and Sergeants Mess HQ UNFICYP

Left to right – S/Sgt Bill Whittie (Britcon), CQMS Tony Byrne (Ircon), Sgt Jim Casey (Ircon), Sgt Patrick Peters (Britcon) at a function in Warrant Officers and Sergeants Mess in 1974.

United Nations soldiers on the Green Line

United Nations M-113 on Patrol

Chapter 8
Crisis 1967

From 1964 up to 1967 there was relative calm between both communities, with sporadic shootings and incidents; these were dealt with by United Nations Forces. In November 1967 the Cypriot Government attempted to introduce patrols into the Turkish enclaves of Ayios Theodhoros, Kophinou and other enclaves by Greek Cypriot Police escorted by Greek Cypriot National Guard. This was resisted by the Turkish Cypriot Fighters. The Greek Cypriot National Guard surrounded both enclaves, attempting to send in armed patrols. On the 15th of November 1967 fighting broke out resulting in the death of twenty-six Turkish Cypriot Fighters and unarmed civilians. The Greek Cypriot National Guard overran most of the enclaves. After Turkey protested to the United Nations Secretary General, they withdrew on the 16th of November 1967.

The Turkish air force strafed Greek Cypriot National Guard positions on the 18th and 19th of November 1967 on numerous occasions and appeared to be readying itself for an intervention. Armed clashes also spread to the Kokkina and Kyrenia areas.

Turkey issued an ultimatum and threatened to intervene in force to protect Turkish Cypriots. Their conditions, were the removal of extra Greek National troops from Cyprus to the strength agreed by Treaty of Alliance August 1960 and cessation of pressure on the Turkish Cypriot community. Once again concern grew, within the NATO membership, for the security of the alliance as a result of the events. There was a potential threat of war between

Greece and Turkey, the situation was descaled when United States became involved in negotiations.

After negotiations under the auspices of the Offices of the United Nations Secretary-General, Greece, Turkey and Cyprus, Greece agreed to withdraw its forces from Cyprus except for the contingent allowed by the 1960 treaties, provided that Turkey did the same and also dismount its intervention force. Turkey agreed, and the crisis passed. During December 1967 and early January 1968, about ten thousand Greek troops were withdrawn.

Capitalising on the agreement the Turkish Cypriots proclaimed their own provisional administration on the 28th of December 1967. President Makarios immediately declared the new administration illegal. Nevertheless, a major change had occurred as a result. Intercommunal talks by all sides took place in an attempt to resolve the situation in 1968, 1969 and 1970 but failed to come to a conclusive agreement by all sides.

Chapter 9

Coup d'Etat the 15th July 1974

Coup d'Etat Greek Military Junta Athens Greece

The Military Junta in Athens Greece was of the opinion that President Makarios was no longer a true supporter of Enosis. They suspected him of being a communist sympathiser and an obstacle to the realization of their enosis objectives. This led the Greek Military Junta supporting EOKA and the Greek Cypriot National Guard, who were controlled by Greek Officers from Greece which undermined the authority of President Makarios. Early July 1974, President Makarios ordered Greece to remove some six hundred and fifty National Greek officers from Cyprus. The Greek Junta's immediate reaction was to order the go-ahead of the coup d'état. On the 15th of July 1974 sections of the Greek Cypriot National Guard, led by its Greek officers, overthrew the government of Cyprus.

Nikos Sampson was declared provisional president of the new government. Prior to the Turkish Intervention, the United States administration gave partial recognition to the Nikos Sampson regime. Sampson was an ultra-nationalist, pro-Enosis combatant who was known to be fanatically anti-Turkish. He had made an open call for a complete genocide of Turkish Cypriots during the sixties, he later claimed that EOKA was "not a threat" to the Turkish Cypriots, after having spent eleven years leading mass murders, not only the Turkish Cypriots, who were the main targets of this vicious campaign, but also fellow Greek Cypriots who were not in favour of enosis (Union with Greece). This act by the Samson regime and the Greek Military Junta in Greece inflamed Turkey and Turkish Cypriots sensibilities. The Sampson regime took over radio stations and declared that President Makarios had been killed, with Makarios, safe in London, it was possible to counteract these broadcasts. They also took over government establishments and Nicosia International Airport after defeating the Tactical Reserve Corps, the Greek Cypriot Police, loyal to President Makarios who were stationed in the airport.

Turkey then issued a list of demands to Greece. These demands included the immediate removal of Nikos Sampson, the withdrawal of six hundred and fifty Greek officers from the Greek Cypriot National Guard. The admission of Turkish troops to protect their population, equal rights for both populations, and access to the sea from the northern coast for Turkish Cypriots and to return Cyprus to its neutral status.

Nicosia International Airport

Stricken Tourists – Nicosia Airport

At 07.00 hours on my way to HQ UNFICYP on the 15th of July 1974. I personally observed the Greek Cypriot National Guard taking up positions on both sides of the main road to the Airport and around the perimeter of the airport. There were volleys of small arms fire from time to time. The exchange of fire was between the Greek Cypriot National Guard and the Greek Cypriot Police (Tactical Reserve Force "Efedriko") stationed in the Airport. On arrival at HQ UNFICYP, I immediately informed the Canadian officer on operations duty, he did not believe this could be happening but I assured him it was. This coup d'état immediately changed the role of United Nations Forces in Cyprus. The attempt surprised President Makarios however, poor execution by the coup d'état organisers gave him time to escape to Paphos. The UN Secretary General had ordered UNFICYP to guarantee the President's safety. President Makarios was then whisked to the Sovereign base of Akrotiri in southern Cyprus where he was then evacuated via Malta to London.

Nicosia City

At 07.00 hours on the 15th of July 1974 a column of fourteen Greek Cypriot National Guard T-34 medium tanks armed with 85mm guns plus .50 calibre machine guns, with a crew of four in each and six BTR-152 armoured personnel carriers armed with the Goryunov 7.62mm co-axial machine guns and an estimated eighteen Greek Cypriot National Guard soldiers in each vehicle, drove through the airport roundabout three kilometres from HQ UNFICYP and Nicosia International Airport, heading towards Nicosia city centre. Two T-34 medium tanks remained at the airport roundabout. At irregular intervals, they fired their .50 calibre machine guns into the air.

At 07.20 hours the remainder of the column engaged the Presidential Palace burning it almost to ruins by 08.00 hours, President Makarios escaped as the palace was being attacked. The House of Representatives, the Paphos Gate Police Station, the Athalassa Tactical Reserve Unit (TRU) HQ and the Cyprus Broadcasting Corporation were taken over. The radio station continually played military music throughout the day, on numerous occasions it announced that President Makarios had been killed.

At 10.00 hours three BTR-152s with Greek Cypriot National Guard arrived at the airport, attacked the Greek Cypriot Tactical Reserve Corps (Greek Cypriot Police). Initially they offered a strong resistance, but their small arms were no match for the attackers and a number were killed or wounded. By noon the Greek Cypriot National Guard were in full control of the airport terminal building, the airport complex and also Nicosia city. As a result, Nicosia airport was closed to civilian traffic. On the 18th and 19th of July 1974 it was allowed to reopen to civilian traffic, becoming a site of chaotic scenes as frightened holidaymakers and other foreign nationals arranged to leave the island.

That afternoon there was only sporadic fighting and an attack on the Archbishops residence. It is believed the airport was strengthened by Greek Cypriot National Guard and Greek Regiment (ELDYK) during the afternoon.

News of the Coup D'état Reactions

As news of the coup d'état spread around the world, the issue of Cyprus returned to centre-stage at the United Nations HQ New York. Threats abounded between the Turkish, Greek, and Cypriot delegations as they each blamed each other.

On the 15th of July of 1974, immediately after the coup d'état, the America aircraft carrier "America", proceeded to the western area off the Cyprus coast. The carriers "Independence" and "Forrestal" joined immediately after.

The Russians then deployed their missile cruiser "Grozny" and anti-submarine ship "Red Caucasus" to patrol the western sea off the island. The destroyer "Flame" to patrol the sea to the south. The minesweeper "Rear Admiral

Pershin" to patrol the sea in the northern area. The "admirals Nakhimov" and "Makarov" to patrol the sea in eastern area. Also the "Abakan" was deployed to the area from Piraeus in Greece to monitor radio transmissions.

On the 18th of July, the situation escalated when the Soviet Union entered the fray by officially blaming NATO and the Greek Military Junta government in Athens Greece for trying to conceal its involvement in this "criminal act". Soviet pressure dramatically raised the stakes and Cyprus became a potential cold war battleground for the superpowers. After four days of unproductive negotiations, British and American negotiators failed to find a solution that would meet with the approval of all parties and the talks fell apart.

The coup d'état led to a surge in intercommunal violence between Greek and Turkish Cypriots, with each side fearing for their own safety and interests.

The rise of the Greek Military junta and the subsequent coup d'état in Cyprus greatly exacerbated the tensions between Greek and Turkish Cypriots. The Junta's push for enosis and its actions to remove President Makarios from power set in motion a chain of events that ultimately led to the Turkish intervention.

The coup d'état not only destabilized the fragile political balance in Cyprus, but also provided Turkey with a justification to intervene militarily. In the aftermath, the division between the two communities deepened, and the consequences of the coup d'état and subsequent intervention continue to shape the island's political landscape to this day.

The Greek Cypriot National Guard made no attempts to enter the Turkish enclaves during the coup d'état. They raided Turkish Cypriot homes in mixed villages to confiscate weapons. A few cases of firing into the Turkish enclave north of Nicosia were reported, the firing was stopped through liaison with the Greek Cypriot National Guard and HQ UNFICYP.

The number of Greek Cypriots killed or missing is in dispute, as some may have been included in the Turkish Intervention numbers. It is surmised that three hundred Greek Cypriot civilians were killed and thirty Greek Officers (ELDYK), with approximately one thousand six hundred and seventeen Greek Cypriots missing.

On the 19th of July, President Makarios attended a United Nations Security Council meeting in New York and gave a speech, in which he stated that *"Cyprus had been invaded by Greece, which violated the independence and sovereignty of the Republic"*.

Chapter 10

The Turkish "Intervention" or "Invasion"

Treaty of Guarantee

On granting independence to Cyprus, a Treaty of Guarantee was signed on the 16th of August 1960 by United Kingdom of Great Britain and Northern Ireland, Greece, Turkey and Cyprus. I refer to the following articles: -

Article I - States

"The Republic of Cyprus undertakes to ensure the maintenance of its independence, territorial integrity and security, as well as respect for its Constitution. It undertakes not to participate, in whole or in part, in any political or economic union with any State whatsoever. It accordingly declares prohibited any activity likely to promote, directly or indirectly, either union with any other State or partition of the Island."

My opinion, The Cyprus government was constantly in breach of this article by its involvement in attempting union with Greece and Enosis policies, the attempt to modify the constitution in 1963. The coup d'état on the 15th of July 1974 was also a major factor which was condemned by United Nations Security Council on the 29th of July 1974 under resolution 573 and also President Makarios at a United Nations Security Council meeting.

Article IV. States

"In the event of a breach of the provisions of the present Treaty, Greece, Turkey and the United Kingdom undertake to consult together with respect to the

representations or measures necessary to ensure observance of those provisions. In so far as common or concerted action may not prove possible, each of the three guaranteeing Powers reserves the right to take action with the sole aim of re-establishing the state of affairs created by the present Treaty".

My opinion, Turkey had the right to intervene to restore the pre-coup d'état democratic regime under article IV. This was confirmed under the above resolution 573 mentioned in article I. Resolution 573 also called on Turkey, as a signatory state, "to guarantee the sovereignty, territorial integrity and security of Cyprus." Turkey was in breach of Article I- by partition of the Island.

A Turkish delegation flew to London on the 17th of July 1974 to demand that Britain fulfil her responsibilities under the Treaty of Guarantee. Despite their military Sovereign Base Areas on the island, Britain choose not to act.

Britain in my opinion had a right to intervene, she had a moral obligation to do so, she had the military capacity to intervene. She did not intervene for reasons the government did not wish to disclose. It may have been its commitment to Northern Ireland at the time, with fifteen thousand troops deployed there and the re-introduction of direct rule of Ulster from Westminster. This may have been a deciding factor in not intervening. Many conspiracy theorists have claimed different reasons. The copy of a telegram sent to Canberra Australia by British Foreign and Commonwealth Office on the 21st of July 1974 speaks for its self.

Copy Page 1 of Telegram sent by Foreign and Commonwealth London UK.

"O. LH13267 JG2   TOR 0749
O. LH13267 2130 21.7.74
To. Canberra /10734
CC. Athens/85 Ankara/65
From. London
SECRET Cyprus: British Policy

1. *You will have seen media reports of Turkish Invasion of Cyprus on 20th July. FCO spokesman has summarized British objectives as being threefold: to protect British lives and property; put pressure on Turkey to stop the fighting and on Greece to do nothing to make matters worse; and to get takes [sic: talks] started in London.*
2. *Commenting privately to us on the situation on 20 July a senior FCO official said that Britain secretly would not object if Turkish military forces occupied about 1/3 of the island before agreeing to a ceasefire. (Please protect). Such a position would need to be reached by 21 July if peace prospects were not to be endangered further. In the meantime, Britain continued to support publicly appeals for an immediate ceasefire.*
3. *According to the same source reports from the British Ambassador in Athens express concern that the present military regime in Greece may fall and be replaced by an even less desirable one. There is some feeling on the FCO that were Greece to intervene militarily in a land war with Turkey she would end up with a "bloody nose".*
4. *In his London talks last week Makarios asked the British frankly what he should do. He was encouraged to go ahead with his plan to go to New York and await developments there. There seems little prospect of his returning to Cyprus in the near future, if at all. Some observers have suggested the President of the Cypriot National Assembly as a possible alternative Head of State to Sampson who is unacceptable to the Turkish.*
5. *Britain is acting diplomatically, not militarily [sic: militarily], in the current crisis. The only military moves have been related strictly to the improvement of the security of the Sovereign Base Areas (SBAs). Over the last 24 hours some 1500 British troops have been flown to Cyprus for this purpose".*

While there is no explicit answer as to why this information was communicated to Australia, the deployment of the Australian Police Contingent (AUSTICIVPOL) serving with UNFICYP, probably explains why the FCO chose to privately brief Australian authorities, passing on information on the secret views of the British Government.

Turkish Landings

Parachute Drop – North Nicosia

Landings Pentemili

On the 20th of July 1974, the Turkish Prime Minister thanked the British and American negotiators but announced on Turkish radio, that the Turkish Armed Forces had started landing in Cyprus to assist the Turkish Cypriot population. The Turkish action was imminent, with dangerous implications for the NATO alliance. It did not take long for the attack to materialize as Turkish fighter jets pounded Greek Cypriot National Guard encampments, towns, villages, Nicosia city and Nicosia International Airport, while they also protected their aircraft dropping paratroopers onto the plains north of Nicosia and the airport. When the Turkish naval vessels held their position at Pentemili five miles west of Kyrenia at 07.30 hours HQ UNFICYP believed that the Turkish Forces intended to secure the Kyrenia harbour for an incursion deeper into Cyprus. It was surmised that they intended to link and control the Kyrenia road, from Kyrenia via the Turkish Cypriot Enclave of Bogaz pass to the Guyeli Enclave of North Nicosia city.

The Turkish assault on Cyprus placed HQ UNFICYP in the centre of an expanding war zone. The HQs location adjacent to the strategically important Nicosia International Airport, being the major factor of the Turkish objectives. The combination of Turkish strafing runs and mortar barrages from both sides put HQ UNFICYP personnel continuously in the line of fire, resulting in a number of direct hits and casualties.

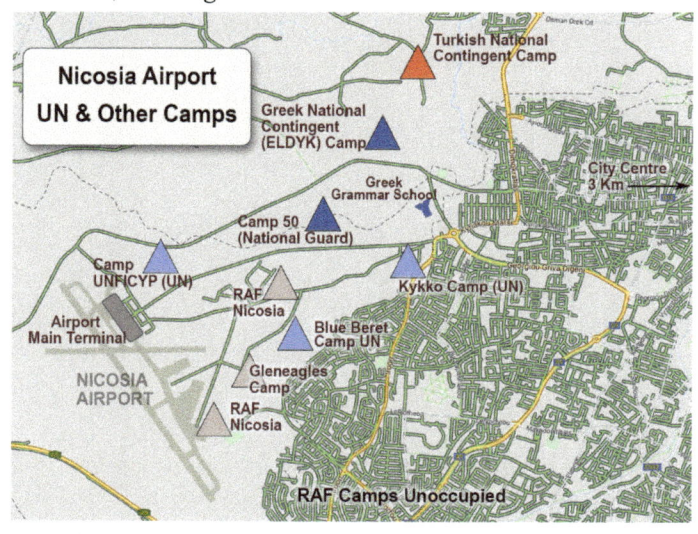

Location - UN Camps - UNFICYP - Blue Beret -Kykko - RAF Nicosia Camps were vacated in 1974.

Operation Attila

The intervention began on the 20th of July 1974, Turkey launched Operation Attila, a full-scale military intervention in Cyprus. The ground forces detailed for the operation were put under the command of the 6th Corp/Second Army. They included the "Cakmak Special Strike Force", a brigade level unit which would conduct the amphibious landing, the 50th Infantry Regiment, the Commando Brigade, the Parachute Brigade, the 39th Infantry Division plus one company of 39th Division Tank Battalion, the 28th Motorised Infantry Division and elements of the 5th Armoured Brigade. The initial landing force was approximately three thousand soldiers. The final total strength eventually reached forty thousand Turkish troops, about six thousand Turkish Cypriot Fighters and the Turkish Regiment (KTKA) made up the intervention force.

Their intervention initially targeted Kyrenia, a key coastal town in the northern part of the island. Turkish Forces advanced, overwhelming Greek Cypriot National Guard defences and capturing strategic positions.

Turkey's powerful air force and navy played a crucial role in the success of the intervention. Turkish air superiority allowed them to strike targeted locations, while their naval dominance secured supply lines and facilitated troop movement. This superiority placed Greek Cypriot National Guard at a huge significant disadvantage.

The Turkish Armed Forces implemented a well-coordinated plan of attack, advancing and occupying key areas in Northern Cyprus. Their primary objective was to secure territory predominantly inhabited by Turkish Cypriots, pushing Greek Cypriot National Guard and civilians to retreat southward.

Resistance efforts by Greek Cypriot National Guard, though valiant, were ultimately overwhelmed by the Turkish military's superior numbers, weaponry, Air Force and Navy.

At times the Turkish Forces advance was slow but remorseless. Observers, were astonished at the huge casualty losses Turkish units were prepared to take, in achieving their objectives.

Greek Cypriot National Guard units were bombed and strafed before they got to the fighting areas and suffered heavy losses of both men and equipment.

Their co-ordination was poor among their widely dispersed units and even when defensive blocks were established. Morale was low among some of the scattered Greek Cypriot National Guard units this was also a factor. Although some units fought bravely, particularly the artillery which was well handled, at the end many reservist units deserted en masse.

Greek Cypriot National Guard and ELDYK Regiment Deployment

They were divided into three sectors: "western", "central" and "eastern". Their plan was to delay the Turkish Forces advancement to the west and east, while retreating to the main defence line (the Troodos Line), and hold positions on the centre. The main defence line, also called Troodos line, was the defence line where they would stand and fight. Until then, their units were ordered to fight flexibly, retreating when needed to do so. The Troodos line left about 40% of the island, including Famagusta, accessible to the Turkish Force.

The western sector was defended by the 11th Tactical Group. Its left flank north was at the sea, near Vasileia (1), and its right south at the United Nations positions around the International Airport of Nicosia (7). The 11th Tactical Guard consisted of the following battalions: 256th centred around ELDYK's 1st company at Vasileia, 316th (reinforced with part of the 366th Reserve Battalion) at Kornos (2), 281st (reinforced with one company of the 286th) at Kontemenos (3), 231st (with the rest of the 286th) at Skylloura (4), the 216th at Gerolakkos (5) and the 33MK Commando at Hill 350, near

Kalo Chorio (6), on the Agia Marina pass. Nicosia International Airport was held by a large combined force of ELDYK reinforcements (A 35MK Commando) as well as a company of the 286th Battalion, and a company of Greek Cypriot paramilitary police.

1. Vasileia
2. Kornos
3. Kontemenos
4. Skylloura
5. Geralakkos
6. Kalo Chorio
7. Nicosia Airport
8. Mia Millia
9. Pentedaktylos
10. Mountains
11. Kyrenia
12. Nicosia
13. Famagusta.

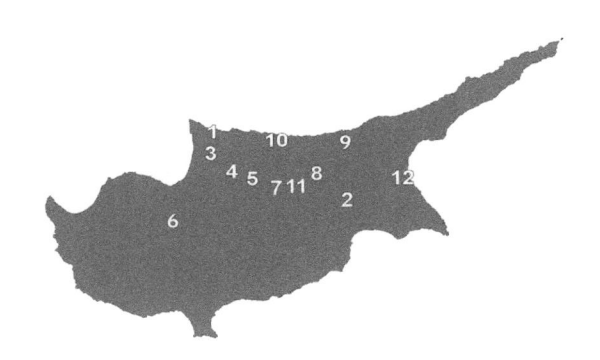

The central sector spread from Nicosia International Airport and ended at the suburb of Nicosia at Mia Milia (8). It consisted of, the 212th Reserve Battalion, ELDYK's camp detachment (three companies), the 336th Reserve Battalion (reinforced with various companies, and with a total strength of one thousand three hundred men), the 211th Battalion and the 187th Artillery Battalion.

The eastern flank was the strongest sector, where the weight of the Turkish attack was expected to fall. It was defended by the DAT (Eastern Sector Command), which consisted of the 12th Tactical Group and the 9th Tactical Group. Further to the east were positioned the 1st High Tactical Command and the 15th Tactical Group. The 9th Tactical Group lay north, from the sea and including the Pentedaktylos mountains (9) and the 12th south of the mountains until and including Mia Milia village. From north to south the units were: The 9th TG, 361st Battalion, 32 MK Commando and 346th Battalion on reserve. The 12th Tactical Group, 251st Battalion (reinforced with one Reserve Company), the 305th Reserve Battalion (aka "Markou's group" with one hundred and fifty soldiers), the 399th Battalion, and the 241st Battalion on reserve. Independent units included the 398th Battalion facing the Turkish Cypriot enclave of Tziaos and the 226th Battalion in general reserve. The total size of the Greek Cypriot National Guard and National Greek Forces numbered at around twenty thousand soldiers, eighteen thousand Greek National Guard, two thousand Greek National soldiers and (ELDYK).

In my opinion, the Greek Cypriot National Guard Command made an extraordinary disastrous blunder; their order of battle was theoretically equal to the Turkish Forces. With up to thirty thousand soldiers under arms, thirty-two T-34 medium tanks and excellent, although mixed calibre, artillery units, the Greek Cypriot National Guard could have possibly contained the two beleaguered bridgeheads. Their mistake was twofold, first, their planning assumed that Turkish Forces would try and seize the harbour and docks at Famagusta (12) on the east coast. Second, many of the Greek Cypriot National Guard units had been dispersed around the island to deal with any opposition to the recent coup d'état. Instead of concentrating their forces to meet the Turkish Forces, directly and as quickly as possible, which should have been the clear military priority tactic. They ordered key dispersed units to ignore the Turkish landings and over-run the Turkish Cypriot enclaves around the island at Gunyeli, Limassol, Larnaca, Paphos and Famagusta. It was a disastrous strategic military mistake by not fully concentrating on the main objective, fighting the Turkish Intervention Forces, instead of taking on two tasks at the same time.

UNFICYP - Full Alert

On the 20th of July, UNFICYP was placed on full alert. An increased level of observation was maintained throughout the entire island and additional precautions were taken to safeguard isolated Turkish Cypriot villages and enclaves. The Greek Cypriot National Guard reacted to the Turkish Forces operations with strong simultaneous attacks in other parts of the island against most of the Turkish Cypriot enclaves and villages. The best UNFICYP could achieve under the circumstances was to arrange local ceasefires to prevent further loss of life and damage to property. The Turkish Cypriot Fighters, were mainly deployed to protect enclaves and isolated villages, they were heavily outnumbered by the Greek Cypriot National Guard and EOKA B forces.

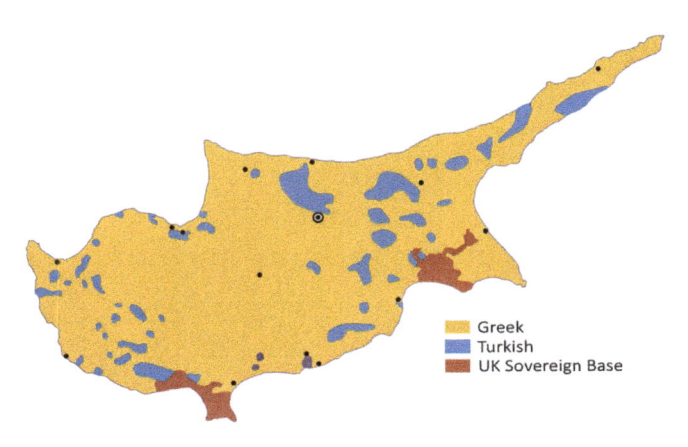

Ethnic Population distribution 1974

Chapter 11
The 20th July 1974

This day marked a watershed moment in the history of Cyprus, it was caught in the midst of a bitter conflict that would forever shape its destiny.

Kyrenia Area

Kyrenia is a town on the northern coast. It is noted for its historic harbour and castle. Home to a beautiful crescent-shaped harbour front and some stunning sandy beaches. Kyrenia was one of the leading tourist resorts on the Northern coastline of Cyprus. In 1974 it had a mixed percentage population of 67.7% inhabitants who were Greek Cypriots, Turkish Cypriots made up 25.1% of the population and other residents 7.2%.

Kyrenia Harbour

The town's inhabitants, Greek Cypriots, Turkish Cypriots, Maronite, Armenian, Latin and British coexisted and cooperated in their daily affairs.

At 05.00 hours, two Greek Cypriot Naval motor torpedo boats P-4 skinheads, the T-1 and T-3, were dispatched from Kyrenia harbour to engage the Turkish naval vessels which had been detected at 04.30 hours approaching 12 miles off the coastline of Cyprus. The T-1 was hit by 40mm anti-aircraft fire and sank. A few minutes later, the T-3 was destroyed by combined fire from Turkish naval ships and fighter aircraft, it sank with the loss of all but one of its crewmembers. The rest of the Cyprus Navy vessels were sunk by their own crews at Naval base "Chrysulis" in Boghazi in order that they could not be used by the Turkish Forces.

At 06.00 hours the Turkish Forces launched an amphibious operation at Pentemili beach, located on the northern coastline, eight kilometres west of the main harbour town of Kyrenia.

Pentemili Beach

The Turkish Naval Force involved in transporting the amphibious forces originated from Mersin port in Turkey and had first attempted to land at the beach of Glykiotissa, but this beach proved inappropriate for a beachhead, this was a major error by the Turkish Forces leaving them five to eight kilometres from their original target.

This force consisted of around three thousand troops, twelve M-47/48 tanks and twenty M-113 armoured personnel carriers, as well as twelve 105mm howitzers, plus personal weapons. The landings were not contested until the first wave of Turkish Forces were already ashore. The Greek Cypriot National Guard had taken some of their T-34 medium tanks which were based in Kyrenia to Nicosia on the 15th of July 1974 to assist in the coup d'état, this drastically weakened their firepower, until the tanks returned.

At 09.00 hours the Greek Cypriot National Guard 251st Infantry Battalion aided by 23rd Tank Battalion Platoon of five T-34 medium tanks, were the first to engage the Turkish landing force, assisted with sporadic artillery support from nearby artillery battalions. The attack initially resulted in the destruction of two Turkish anti-tank recoilless rifles, M-40A1 100mm and M-18A1-57 of the Turkish Cakmak Special force by fire from Greek Cypriot National Guard T-34 medium tanks and infantry support. A number of casualties were inflicted on the Turkish Forces, but the attack was unsuccessful in dislodging the beachhead force. At 11.00 hours, a Turkish counter-attack, supported by M-113 armoured personnel carriers and air support, resulted in the destruction of five Greek Cypriot National Guard T-34 medium tanks of the 23rd Tank Battalion by Turkish light anti-tank weapons. Two Turkish M-113 armoured personnel carriers having difficulty coming ashore were destroyed by Greek Cypriot National Guard T-34 medium tank anti-tank fire. The Greek Cypriot National Guard then retreated south east towards Kyrenia under heavy fire. The Turkish Forces advanced 1km to the east towards Kyrenia town and west towards Morphou.

During the morning air-attacks continued against Greek Cypriot National Guard positions in and around Kyrenia area, with the Greek Cypriot National Guard army camp being strafed, knocking out two Marmon-Herrington Mk-IVF armoured vehicles and a Daimler Dingo fighting vehicle. The local football stadium at Kyrenia was also attacked, destroying two armoured personnel carriers BTR-152's.

Greek Cypriot National Guard artillery units involved in action with the Turkish beachhead were deployed with twelve 25-pounder guns and six anti-aircraft guns of 12.5mm and 14.5mm. The unit abandoned two guns at its camp, due to lack of tractors. On the Lapithou to Kyrenia road, Greek Cypriot National Guard 182nd Artillery Battalion lost two 25 pounder artillery guns in a road accident.

From firing positions at Saint Pavlos, the Greek Cypriot National Guard 190th Battalion fired shots at the Turkish beachhead and in turn, took casualties from naval and air attacks during the day. They had eighteen anti-tank guns of 57mm but only twelve tractors to move them. They abandoned their position at 17.15 hours and were attacked by Turkish aircraft, without any losses. They then divided into two formations of six guns and attacked Turkish Forces at Panagron, and also shot at the Turkish beachhead at Pentemili, forcing Turkish naval vessels to briefly retreat back out to sea, temporarily.

The 191st Greek Cypriot National Guard artillery company engaged the Turkish Forces from its firing positions at Bellapais, resulting in Turkish Forces casualties. The 198th Greek Cypriot National Guard artillery company, equipped with four guns of 75mm and six anti-aircraft guns, was based in the western Kyrenia mountains. This unit had sustained the loss of vehicles, radios and ammunition in a forest fire on the 16th of July, and was in poor shape when it engaged Turkish paratroopers at Saint Hilarion castle on the 20th of July, in support of mountain commando forces in the area gaining no advantage.

Two Greek Cypriot National Guard battalions, the 281st Infantry Battalion and the 286th Mechanised Infantry Battalion plus three T-34 medium tanks were sent from Nicosia to reinforce the defences at Kyrenia, but both were attacked by Turkish aircraft at the village of Kontemnos, resulting in the destruction of soft-skin vehicles, six BTR-152 armoured vehicles, and the killing of the commander of the 286th Battalion. The 316th Battalion was sent from Morphou along the road to Kyrenia, only to be ambushed and forced into defensive positions at a Turkish roadblock. The 316th Battalion then regrouped and joined forces with elements of the 286th Battalion equipped with three T-34 medium tanks which had now arrived.

At 10.00 hours in response to the intervention, a Greek Cypriot National Guard senior staff officer, was sent in an armed motorcade to the western area of Kyrenia in an effort to coordinate a counter-attack and prevent the Turkish Forces from forming a bridgehead to north Nicosia. His plan was to engage the Turkish Forces at night on the western front, using all the available elements of Greek Cypriot National Guard Battalions, along with a unit of anti-tank rifles, three T-34 medium tanks and mortars. The attack commenced at 02.30 hours by the 286th Infantry Battalion and was successful initially, in forcing a temporary retreat by the Turkish Forces, but this resulted in a counter-attack by Turkish Forces. One of the three Greek Cypriot National Guard Boufas Battle Group T-34 medium tanks was hit by a Turkish LAW anti-tank fire and knocked out. At its right flank, the 281st Battalion failed to overrun the first Turkish lines and withdrew. On the eastern flank the 306th Infantry Battalion arrived late and commenced its attack, which did not succeed, they failed to gain any ground and withdrew. On the southern flank, the 316th Infantry Reserve Battalion, which was created by surplus reservists, arrived with no information of the enemy's location. At some point during the night, as it was marching northwards, they realized that the battalion had entered the Turkish lines. After an exchange of fire, the battalion managed to exit the Turkish ambush, and assume defensive positions. The battalion lost a total of seven to ten men killed and wounded, including its commander. During the rest of the night, many of its reservists deserted southwards, back to Nicosia. The battalion eventually disbanded.

During the day the Greek Cypriot population, estimated to be around two thousand six hundred and fifty, fled Kyrenia, seeking refuge in the south. During the operation the Turkish Air force lost in action over Kyrenia and Nicosia areas, two fighter jets F-100 Super Sabre, one aircraft RF-84F and one aircraft Dornier Do-28-D from Greek Cypriot National Guard anti-aircraft fire.

Also three Turkish transport aircraft were damaged by Greek Cypriot National Guard anti-aircraft fire. All were salvaged but not used for any further operations during the conflict.

Nicosia City and Nicosia International Airport

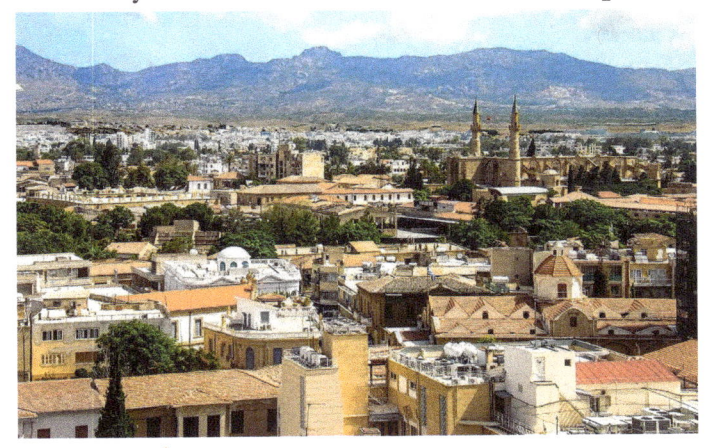

Nicosia City

Nicosia, the capital of Cyprus, stands as a city of contrasts, where ancient walls encircle bustling modern streets and where history meets contemporary life. It lies along the Pedieos River, in the centre of the Mesaoria plain between the Kyrenia mountains north and the Troodos range south. Greek Cypriots made up eighty per cent of the population and Turkish Cypriots eighteen per cent. The remaining two per cent are Latins, Armenians and

Maronites, who at the time of independence opted to belong to the Greek Cypriot community. Since 1964 Nicosia was divided into Greek and Turkish Cypriots sectors. The dividing line, which cuts through the city, was called the Green Line.

Just before 05.00 hours, the battle began in Nicosia when Greek Cypriot National Guard anti-aircraft guns opened up on flights of Turkish aircraft flying in from the north over the Kyrenia mountain range.

At 05.30 hours approximately, one hundred and twenty Turkish paratroopers were dropped from C-130 Hercules, OC-3 and C-160 Transalls, onto the plains north of Nicosia. The operation of parachute drops continued throughout the morning, bringing an estimated total to one thousand. The parachute drops were protected by Turkish air force F-100 Super Sabre jets. Their main objective appeared to be securing the road between north Nicosia and Kyrenia, on the north coast.

Turkish Air Force jets repeatedly bombed and strafed Greek Cypriot National Guard and Greek Regiment (ELDYK) troop encampments on the outskirts of the capital and near Nicosia International airport. Sustained firing from heavy artillery and light weapons continued throughout the day across the United Nations Green Line that divides the Greek and Turkish Cypriot sectors.

By 06.00 hours fighting began to intensify in Nicosia. Opening with scattered shootings, it soon grew to a crescendo of sustained machine gun and mortar fire. At 06.00 hours forty Greek Cypriot National Guard soldiers from the 1st Company of the 211th Infantry Battalion set up on the roof of the Ledra Palace hotel which is located on the Green Line and mounted a 50mm machine gun. Due to its location a potential seizure of the hotel by Turkish Forces would endanger a takeover of the Republic's nearby administrative centres and key services, such as the courts, the telecommunication authority, the parliament, ministries, and the Central Bank.

At 06.10 hours, when Turkish paratroopers began to descend in the North Nicosia area they were opened fire on from the roof of the hotel. At 06.20 hours the Turkish Forces retaliated hitting the Greek Cypriot National Guard and the surrounding area with bullets, mortar shells, and artillery. This continued until the late evening. Resulting in the death of three Greek Cypriot National Guard soldiers and the wounding of a number. Through negotiations with United Nations, the Turkish Forces threatened to drop napalm and bomb the hotel if the Greek Cypriot National Guard did not leave the roof, they refused this request and remained on the roof.

Around three hundred and eighty civilians, mostly foreign nationals, including women, children, and international media representatives, were trapped in the hotel and were located in the basement for safety.

The Turkish jets, continued their bombing runs throughout the morning. They drew increasingly heavy antiaircraft fire, but none were seen downed. The crashing bombs and rockets sent up tall columns of black and grey smoke. By mid-morning, the smoke had formed a haze that obscured the outskirts of the city and the beautiful blue skies of Cyprus.

Nicosia International Airport prior to 1974

The Battle for Nicosia International Airport

The Battle for Nicosia Airport commenced on the 20th of July 1974 to 24th of July1974. It became a fierce battleground during the conflict between the Greek Cypriot National Guard, (ELDYK) and the Turkish Forces, with United Nations personnel in the middle. Control of the airport held significant importance for both sides, offering a vital vantage point and a gateway for military reinforcements.

As the battle unfolded, intense fighting erupted with heavy artillery, tank fire, and airstrikes. The Greek Cypriot National Guard fiercely defended their positions, while the Turkish Forces sought to gain control of the airport. The conflict showcased the devastating power of modern warfare, death, tearing apart buildings and causing immense destruction.

The battle spanned five days, with both sides locked in brutal combat. The airport's runways became pockmarked with craters, rendering them unusable for civilian and military purposes.

Ultimately, on the 24th of July, the ceasefire of the 21st of July was recognised by the Turkish Forces, bringing an end to the intense fighting temporarily. The airport would never regain its former status as a bustling hub of connectivity, as it is in ruins. The scars of this battle would act as a sombre reminder of the deep wounds inflicted during the Cyprus conflict.

The Nicosia Airport battle marked a significant turning point in the division of Cyprus, solidifying the divide between the Greek Cypriots south and the Turkish Cypriots north. The conflict resulted in thousands of displaced individuals and had a lasting socio-political impact on the island.

Today, the remains of the Nicosia Airport serve as a haunting memorial, a testament to the tragedy of war and a reminder of the need for peaceful resolution. The events are detailed below as they occurred on a daily basis.

At 06.30 hours the Turkish Air force with F- 100 Super Sabres, began dropping their bombs, rockets and napalm in Nicosia on the camp of the

Greek Cypriot National Guard and Greek Regiment (ELDYK) close to the Grammar School. They then commenced bombing the airport heavily and a ground attack of multiple battalions also ensued at a later date. Most of the damage caused by the air strikes at the airport was the cratering of the runway in a number of locations and windows blasted out from the main terminal building. The F-100 super sabre aircraft began to locate the artillery batteries of the Greek Cypriot National Guard which they continued bombing until late evening.

At about the same time, it was learned that the Turkish Air Force was preparing to attack the Nicosia hospital since anti-aircraft artillery of the Greek Cypriot National Guard was on the roof of the building. In fact, there were two .50 calibre weapons. HQ UNFICYP were able to convince the Greek Cypriot National Guard officer in charge to remove themselves, this resulted in the attack being averted.

By midday seven waves of paratroopers were dropped and three loads of men were landed by helicopter in order to finally place the Airborne Brigade on the plain north of Nicosia. They joined with the Turkish Cypriot Fighters who were operating in the area. Exchanges of fire between the Greek Cypriot National Guard located at the airport, grammar school and other locations took place spontaneously.

At 06.20 hours, Turkish air force attacked Camp Andrew Greek Cypriot National Guard 185th Artillery Battalion in Nicosia. Using rockets and napalm, five 25 pounder artillery weapons were destroyed with the death of six Greek Cypriot National Guard soldiers plus a number injured.

At 06.45 hours, a massive Turkish air force attack commenced on Camp Dimitri, Athalassa Nicosia, location of the Greek Cypriot National Guard 187th Artillery Battalion. This resulted in the destruction of eight 25 pounder artillery weapons and the death of six Greek Cypriot National Guard soldiers plus a number injured.

At 07.00 hours a battalion of five hundred and fifty Greek Cypriot National Guard and (ELDYK), supported by nineteen T-34 medium tanks of the 23rd Medium Tank Battalion and one Greek Cypriot National Guard company commenced an attack on the Turkish enclave of Geunyeli, just north-west of Nicosia. Geunyeli was a strategic target due to its position controlling the Nicosia-Kyrenia main road, it had to be captured by the Greek Cypriot National Guard in order to ensure reinforcements to Kyrenia. This enclave was heavily fortified by the Turkish Cypriot Fighters, in preparation for just such a siege, and was protected by bunkers, machine gun nests and anti-tank trenches. Positioned within the enclave was the Geunyeli Group of the contingent of the (KTKA) Turkish Army, now strengthened by the Turkish parachute landing force. The attack began with the shelling of Geunyeli by T-34 medium tanks and artillery, which resulted in a Turkish counter attack with air strikes, but because of the prevailing smoke from the bombardment and smoke mortars, these proved to be largely inaccurate. Six armoured personnel carriers BTR-152V1 of Greek Cypriot National Guard 286th Mechanised Infantry Battalion attempted to go through Kontemnos village. They were attacked by Turkish jet fighters all six burst into flames and were destroyed.

An attempt by the Greek Cypriot National Guard to make a direct coordinated attack with their tanks resulted in total disaster, with two T-34 medium tanks destroyed by aircraft attacks, and one T-34 medium tank becoming trapped in an anti-tank ditch. As the battle progressed, Turkish parachutists continued to drop in and around the enclave, leading to some unavoidable casualties, it is alleged that ninety-three were killed or wounded during the drop. The 185th Greek Cypriot National Guard Artillery Battalion, equipped with twelve 25-pounder guns and six anti-aircraft guns (four .50cal and two 14.5mm) moved to its firing positions outside Geunyeli. Before it could commence its attack, it was attacked by the Turkish Air Force, resulting in the loss of five 25-pounder guns and six soldiers. Its remaining guns shelled Geunyeli and then it retreated south west. The 184th Greek Cypriot National Guard Artillery Company, managed to rescue its armament of six 25-pounder guns and two .50cal anti-aircraft guns from its burning base camp following an air attack, as a result three personnel were killed. It initially fired shots at Geunyeli, before moving with the 185th Artillery Battalion. The Greek Cypriot National Guard could make no advancement into the enclave due to heavy resistance and withdrew to the south-west. They called for reinforcements for a second co-ordinated attack using their remaining 15 tanks, and the 361st and 399th Greek Cypriot National Guard Infantry Battalions, these new forces tasked to circling in from the north and east to encircle and destroy the enclave. However, the co-ordinated attack, planned for 18.00 hours, failed to materialise as the 399th Infantry Battalion was delayed by fighting with Turkish Cypriot Fighters. When the 399th Infantry Battalion arrived, it attempted to attack the enclave on its own, but achieved little success and so withdrew.

At 12.15 hours from Kykko Camp and Blue Beret Camp one could see the position of the mortar battery of the Greek Cypriot National Guard in the ravine just south of the camps and the firing of their mortars. To the north the landing and exploding of their shells in the Turkish enclave located 6,000 metres further North at Guenyeli, could also be seen. Immediately the Turkish Forces retaliated with their mortar bombs, which began falling dangerously close to Camp UNFICYP (Britcon) the Blue Beret Camp and directly striking Kykko Camp (Finnish). They also fell beyond the airport road close to the airport.

Kykko Camp after direct mortar strikes

The Greek Cypriot National Guard used United Nations positions as a shield since they had a perfect knowledge of the sectors locations occupied by the United Nations personnel.

The artillery and anti-aircraft units of the Greek Cypriot National Guard were deployed in a ravine located south, beside Blue Beret Camp (Cancon) and Kykko Camp (Fincon). The local commander of Greek Cypriot National Guard was requested by HQ UNFICYP to move his batteries from the ravine south of the United Nations Camps as the camps were in the centre of both warring forces, but he refused to do so.

At 13.00 hours having located some of the batteries of the Greek Cypriot National Guard the Turkish F-104 Star Fighters commenced bombings. Before the attack the pilots jettisoned their reserves and some fell on Blue Beret Camp. It was noted that the F-I04 Star Fighter pilots were more skilful than those of the F-100 Super Sabre. The manoeuvres of the attack were their low-altitude flights, which were made quickly and skilfully. These airstrikes continued until approximately 17.30 hours resulting in the destruction of eight 25 pounder artillery guns at Greek Cypriot National

Guard positions in Nicosia. Also, during this period mortar and machine gun battles continued between both forces.

On the morning of the intervention Comdt. James Flynn (Ircon) was at the National Guard Headquarters in Nicosia and as result he was cut off from returning to HQ UNFICYP. He remained with them for seven days constantly moving location as they moved to evade direct bombings by the Turkish Air Force. We had no contact with him during this period although he did have radio communication with him. I assumed he had to maintain radio silence on instructions from the Greek Cypriot National Guard.

This caused grave concern for his safety among the staff at HQ UNFICYP, especially the Force Commander D. Prem Chand, he spoke personally to me day and night on the situation and he requested I keep calling Comdt. Flynn in the Irish language on the radio. I continually did so but to no avail of a response. I could see from the expression on the Force Commander's face his concern was genuine.

Limassol

Limassol City

Limassol is a city on the southern coast of Cyprus. It is the second largest urban area in Cyprus after Nicosia. It is the main port in Cyprus. In 1974 it had a population in the region of thirty-seven thousand four hundred and eighty Greek Cypriots and six thousand one hundred and twenty Turkish Cypriots in the Turkish enclave. It's the base for many of the island's wine companies, serving the wine-growing regions on the southern slopes of the Troodos Mountains.

At 10.00 hours four hundred and fifty EOKA-B fighters attacked the Turkish Cypriot enclave at Limassol, where approximately one thousand lightly armed Turkish Cypriot Fighters and nine thousand inhabitants were situated. After a brief exchange of gun fire, they surrendered. Following their surrender, it is alleged that the Turkish Cypriot quarter was burned, women raped and children shot. A total of one thousand three hundred Turkish Cypriots were taken as prisoners of war (POWs) and confined in a prison camp.

Paphos

Paphos

Paphos is a coastal town in south west and it lies on the Mediterranean coast, about 50 kilometres (30miles) west of Limassol. In 1974 it had a population of approximately six thousand two hundred and thirty Greek Cypriots in the Greek sector and two thousand eight hundred and fifty Turkish Cypriots in the Turkish enclave. In classical antiquity, two locations were called Paphos, Old Paphos, today known as Kouklia and New Paphos.

At 09.00 hours the Turkish Cypriot enclave was attacked from all sides by Greek Cypriot National Guard and Turkish Cypriot Fighters returned fire. Fierce fighting continued throughout the day with many casualties, the majority on the Turkish Cypriot side.

At around 17.00 hours the Greek landing craft vessel HS Lesvos (L-176) arrived at Paphos and began shelling Turkish-Cypriot positions in the enclave, close to the harbour with her 40mm anti-aircraft guns. Then some four hundred and fifty Greek troops disembarked from the vessel at Paphos, it immediately headed back out to sea to evade the enemy.

At 20.00 hours the Turkish Cypriot Fighters surrendered, and all men of fighting age were taken as prisoners of war.

Famagusta

The Turkish enclave of Famagusta was subjected to heavy shelling by the Greek Cypriot National Guard. As a result, Turkish Cypriot Fighters and Turkish Cypriot civilians took cover behind the walls of the old city and prepared for a siege against Greek Cypriot National Guard, awaiting the arrival of the Turkish Forces.

Village of Alaminos

Alaminos is a village west of Larnaca. This was a mixed village with a population of approximately five hundred and sixty-four Greek Cypriots and two hundred and fifty Turkish Cypriots.

In the afternoon of the 20th of July, it was reported that Greek Cypriot National Guard and EOKA B surrounded the Turkish Cypriot part of the village and ordered it to surrender. The Turkish Cypriot defenders, who were equipped with automatic weapons, refused and opened fire. After a period of sustained shooting, the bulk of the Turkish Cypriot Fighters, about sixty fighters laid down their arms and surrendered due to being drastically outnumbered. They were taken across a bridge that separates the village and were put under guard in the Greek Cypriot schoolhouse. It is alleged five Greek Cypriot National Guard and six Turkish Cypriot Fighters were killed in the fighting. Fourteen Turkish Cypriot fighters were still holding out in a barn but surrendered and were unarmed by EOKA B. It is alleged the fourteen Turkish Cypriot Fighters were taken to a stone stable on the edge of the village. There, they were lined up against a wall of the old stable and shot dead. This report is not confirmed by United Nations, but the bullet holes in the wall of the old stable and a mass grave are evidence of some atrocity. Whatever happened here, the incident was typical of the scores of battles that were fought in the mixed Greek and Turkish Cypriot villages across the island during the opening hours of the Turkish intervention.

While the Greek Cypriot National Guard was taking on the Turkish Forces in a battle on the northern coast of Cyprus, irregular armed bands of Greek and Turkish Cypriots were settling old scores elsewhere on the island. More than anything else, these exchanges revealed the bitterness that divides the Greek and Turkish communities.

Chapter 12
The 21ˢᵗ July 1974

Turkish Air Force Jets Attack Nicosia Airport

Nicosia International Airport

Nicosia International Airport

Nicosia International Airport was the principal airport for Cyprus from its initial construction in the 1930s, it was also used by the Royal Air Force, RAF Nicosia until 1974. In 1949 the first terminal building was designed and built. On the 27th of March 1968 a modern new terminal, was opened. The new terminal could accommodate up to eight hundred passengers at one time and the parking apron could handle eleven aircraft.

At 01.30 hours on the 21st of July 1974, a crisis originated at Nicosia International Airport when 15 Noratlas aircraft from the Greek Hellenic Air Force performed a daring re-supply mission to the Greek Cypriot National Guard in the airport, but due to mechanical problems two had to land in Crete and Rhodes. Of the thirteen aircraft arriving, one aircraft was shot down killing the crew of four and twenty-eight commandos, two were badly shot up and forced to make hard crash landings, killing two commandos and wounding ten and one was damaged on landing. The aircraft were accidently shot down by Greek Cypriot National Guard, who believed they were Turkish aircraft on a bombing mission. The remaining aircraft landed, delivering supplies and an estimated two hundred Greek commandos. All the damaged aircraft were destroyed. The remaining nine aircraft managed to return safely to Greece after unloading their troops and supplies. Perhaps the rationale for doing so was that Greece was not officially at war with Turkey, thus any evidence of Greek involvement in the operations in Cyprus could be erased. The wreckage of the aircraft shot down could be seen from Blue Beret Camp smouldering and burnt out.

This daring action proved that the airport still had strategic value; Greece could potentially re-supply its allies faster than Turkey (which was limited to airdrops, or its new port at Kyrenia harbour). The situation forced the Turkish Forces to remedy the situation quickly. The cost of inaction was to risk losing their gains by further Greek re-supply efforts.

Considering the Turkish position, it is surprising that the dramatic events at the airport did not hamper ceasefire negotiations. By first light, HQ UNFICYP had received assurances from both the liaison negotiators Greek Major Tsolakis and the Turkish Colonel Chakar, that an island-wide ceasefire would be established at 16.00 hours' local time. It is difficult to understand why the Turkish government would choose that moment to accept a ceasefire, except that it possibly believed it could take and occupy most of the airport before the deadline. If so, the Turkish government must have felt that it had met all of its objectives and a ceasefire would solidify their gains. Regardless of the rationale behind the move, the ceasefire became the first sign of improvement in Cyprus since the intervention began. United Nations observation posts throughout the night noted that Turkish Forces tanks were on the move near the Morphou road, the outer boundary north east of the airport. These reports were substantiated when United Nations British Forces at Camp UNFICYP observed Turkish Forces advance units approaching from the north to the airport perimeter. At 11.00 hours the Turkish attack commenced. The assault began by directing aircraft bombing, mortar, rocket, and tank shells towards the main terminal complex, while Turkish soldiers advanced over the flat and open terrain around the airport. During the attack United Nations soldiers received injuries as the Greek Cypriot National Guard and Greek Regiment (ELDYK) were firing over their heads against the Turkish Forces advance and the Turkish Forces firing likewise. The terrain proved fatal for the Turkish offensive as the Greek Cypriot National Guard and ELDKY occupied commanding positions within the control tower and other buildings in the airport. Ricocheting rounds also caused havoc as they ignited the parched fields around the airport in the dry Mediterranean climate. These fires created an unintended natural barrier to the attackers as smoke and flames were disorienting the advancing Turkish Forces.

During their advance Turkish Forces breached the perimeter of Camp UNFICYP. After tense discussions and considerable coaxing, through a mixture of German and French, RSM Birch (the camp's Regimental Sergeant Major) and the Turkish commander finally agreed to leave the camp area and retreated back fifty metres northwards.

After hours of fierce battle during the day, both the Greek Cypriot National Guard and Turkish Forces ceased their operations for the night.

Force Commander Brig. Gen. D Prem Chand and Col. Clayton Beattie Canadian Forces at Kykko Camp (FINCON) after mortar and bombing raid by Turkish Air Force.

Kyrenia

The second wave of Turkish Forces departed from the port of Mersin in Turkey to Cyprus.

The Greek Cypriot National Guard learned that three Turkish Naval destroyers were deployed in the area off the coast of Paphos, carrying out observations on Greek destroyers. The Greek Cypriot National Guard were aware that their radio transmissions were being monitored by the Turkish Forces, they then commenced to continually transmit from a Cyprus Naval station in Paphos, that it was a Greek Naval Force offshore. The false transmissions deception worked, and the Turkish Air Force launched an airstrike against their own destroyers.

It consisted of sixteen F-100D Super Sabres, each carrying two 750- pound bombs, and sixteen F-104G Starfighters, each carrying a single 750-pound bomb. The fighters had no particular problem finding their targets, and attacked immediately, despite the large Turkish flags on the destroyers. The problem was the Greek Navy also operated former USN destroyers, of the Gearing class. The air attack resulted in sinking D-354 Kocatepe with a loss of 54 crew, damaging D-353 Adatepe and D-351 Moresal Fevzi Cakmak which were able to return to port.

In the morning the Greek Cypriot Commander of the Navy, was heading to Karavas to assess the size and dimensions of the Turkish landing force, a team of twelve Turkish parachutists were dropped in the area to ambush his convoy. The Turkish troops managed to wound the Commander before they were wiped out by the commander's personal guard force, forcing the Greek Cypriot plan to be abandoned.

At Kyrenia, the Greek Cypriot National Guard 251st Battalion moved to the village of Trimithi to mount its defence of the town, while the 241st and Engineer Battalion moved east of Kyrenia, with the latter tasked to mining the coastline.

Early afternoon the Agyrta-Nicosia pass assault commenced. The Greek Cypriot National Guard achieved their objectives, with two Mechanised Infantry Battalions, 31st and 33rd arriving from the west to capture the Kotsakagia mountain top, while the 32rd arrived from the east to force a Turkish retreat and capture the pass. In a disastrous strategic move, the three Greek Cypriot National Guard Battalions were ordered to move from the Pentedaktylos mountains, where they had created a virtual blockade across the line of a Turkish bridgehead. Why this disastrous decision was ordered is not known?

The Greek Cypriot National Guard garrison camped in Bellapais was subjected to a Turkish air attack, in which napalm was reportedly used.

It is alleged that two Turkish jet fighters F-104 G1 and F-100 CD2 were lost in action during the day.

The Greek Cypriot Navy ran aground motor torpedo boat P-4 skin head at Boghazi, it was captured by Turkish Forces on the 18th of August 1974.

Greek Cypriot National Guard troops were reported using clearly marked United Nations land rovers and flags, reportedly captured from Finnish UNFICYP troops. Some elements of the Turkish Forces wore blue berets which also caused confusion.

Nicosia City

At 06.30 the battle at the Ledra Palace Hotel restarted again with the Greek Cypriot National Guard firing against the Turkish Forces who were fortified in the surrounding houses across the Green Line in the Turkish area. The Turkish Forces retaliated with mortar fire striking the hotel. Again, through UNFICYP the Turkish Forces threatened to napalm and bomb the hotel if the Greek Cypriot National Guard did not leave the roof. They refused UNFICYP's request to leave their position. After negotiation between the opposing forces, it was agreed that the Ledra Palace Hotel be declared a

United Nations protected area and a no-go area to the opposing forces. After much persuading the Greek Cypriot National Guard vacated the premises. The three hundred and eighty civilians located in the hotel were then evacuated by a Canadian United Nations convoy to safety.

Lefka

Lefka Village

Lefka is a town overlooking Morphou Bay. Lefka was historically a copper mining town. The copper reserves were first mined in the middle bronze age. Since 1960 it was a Turkish enclave with a population of four thousand five hundred and forty Turkish Cypriots.

At 04.45 hours Greek Cypriot National Guard attacked the Turkish enclave of Lefka with mortars and heavy machine guns. At around 10.00 hours the Turkish Cypriot Fighters surrendered.

Limassol

At 06.00 hours all Turkish-Cypriot resistance at Limassol collapsed under the weight of a Greek Cypriot National Guard assault, and approximately one thousand POWs were taken. Also, the Turkish-Cypriot held village of Pileri was captured by Greek Cypriot National Guard around the same time.

Larnaca

Larnaca Seafront

Larnaca is a town on the south east coast. Larnaca International Airport is located south of the town.

It has the second largest commercial port on the island. In 1974 it had a population of fourteen thousand nine hundred and fifteen Greek Cypriots, four thousand Turkish Cypriots in the Turkish enclave and six hundred and ninety-five other residents.

At 08.15 hours in Larnaca, talks for a ceasefire between Greek Cypriot National Guard, Turkish Cypriot Fighters broke down and heavy fighting erupted, with the Greek Cypriot National Guard using artillery and mortar fire. By 10.30 hours Turkish Cypriot Fighters and Turkish Cypriot civilians reportedly began their surrender.

Limnitis

Limnitis village

Limnitis is a coastal village in north-western Cyprus. It is sited twenty metres above sea level, but extends all the way down to the beach. It was a Turkish Cypriot village with a population of three hundred and ninety-six Turkish Cypriots.

At 08.45 hours The Turkish Cypriot enclave of Limnitis was attacked by Greek Cypriot National Guard, high-level bombing, shelling and rockets were fired into the enclave. Turkish Cypriot Fighters returned fire, by 10.00 hours they surrendered due to lack of ammunition and being vastly outnumbered.

Chapter 13

The 22nd July 1974

Kyrenia Area

05.30 hours the second wave of Turkish landing ships reached the beachhead at Pentemili and began unloading M-47 and M-48 main battle tanks as well as supporting equipment. It included a tank company and a mechanised infantry company code named "Bora Task Force". The Greek Cypriot forces in the area are unable to contain the new landing force and retreated towards Kyrenia.

At 11.00 hours the Turkish Forces, Bora Task Force and 50th Regiment proceeded to launch an attack against their primary objective Kyrenia, the main harbour on the northern coast.

This resulted in an onslaught against the Greek Cypriot National Guard, 33rd Mechanised Infantry Brigade, the 306th and 251st Battalions who had limited anti-tank capability, they were forced into full retreat, by the Turkish advance. An intervention by the nearby Greek Cypriot National Guard 241st Battalion, attempting to build a defensive line to the west of Kyrenia, failed, and the Battalion was overrun.

The Turkish advance towards Kyrenia along the northern coastal road west was resisted by two mobile lines of defence bisecting their path. In the first instance, the defence by 33rd Mechanised Brigade were able to achieve the destruction of two Turkish M-47 tanks of the 39th Divisional Tank Battalion, which they knocked out with 106mm recoilless rifles. The failure to hold the Turkish Force back, meant that the second line of defence the 241st Battalion was swiftly impacted, they immobilised a third Turkish M-47 tank with an anti-tank rocket and a further two during the attack. Turkish Forces lost five T-47 tanks with twenty-three casualties during the assault. The Greek Cypriot National Guard lost one armoured vehicle ATS-712, destroyed by Turkish fire.

The fast and aggressive nature of the Turkish assault enabled Turkish Forces to enter Kyrenia and then they divided into two separate forces, one to establish a new beachhead in the Kyrenia harbour. The second force headed south to Boghaz pass to unite with a Paratrooper Battalion who had landed there.

It is alleged that Turkish Air Force lost one fighter jet F-100 D2 to anti-aircraft fire. At 14.30 hours United Nations troops had to reluctantly abandon their Camp Tjiklos in the Kyrenia district with refugees under their supervision due to heavy fighting and forest fires.

At 17.00 hours a solid bridgehead had been formed between Kyrenia and the centrally located village of Geunyeli, the latter strategically positioned on the Kyrenia-Nicosia road. The Turkish-Cypriot fortified base at Geunyeli was now under the full control of the Turkish Forces with access from Kyrenia to Turkish enclave in north Nicosia. The last defences at Kyrenia had collapsed. The Greek Cypriot National Guard trapped in the area somehow managed to escape to safety in the south.

Famagusta

At 14.00 hours the Greek Cypriot National Guard 199th Artillery Company, equipped with four guns of 3.7-inch (94mm) and two .50 calibre anti-aircraft guns, commenced an artillery assault against the Turkish Cypriot enclave of the old city of Famagusta, in support of 201st and 386th Battalions. This assault continued for two days, resulting in the Turkish Cypriots taking refuge in the area, awaiting arrival of the Turkish Forces.

Nicosia

At 15.00 hours the Turkish air force launched an exceptionally low level strike on the airport scoring nine direct hits on the runways. At 16.45 hours (after the agreed time of the ceasefire) there was another spectacular action. A flight of six F-104 Starfighters followed by two F-100 Super Sabres attacked the airport and nearby artillery Greek Cypriot National Guard positions. Twenty bombs hit the runways, destroying a Cyprus Airway Trident Jet and other aircraft. Two bombs and some napalm fell short and hit Camp UNFICYP wounding a United Nations British soldier and starting a massive fire in the area.

The Greek Cypriot National Guard 189th Artillery Battalion, equipped with eight guns of 100mm and six anti-aircraft guns (4 x .50cal, 2 x 14.5mm), operated from Camp "Christ Samaritan" in Nicosia, close to the airport, continued with a heavy artillery assault against the Turkish Forces located in Geunyeli and shot against Turkish helicopters in the area. This battalion was repeatedly bombed by the Turkish Air Force, with no losses and held their positions until the 23rd of July 1974.

The Turkish Forces now controlled a narrow area 3% of the island. They successfully achieved their objective by connecting their beachhead in the north with the Turkish Cypriot enclave north of Nicosia city. They controlled the harbour of Kyrenia town and the Kyrenia Nicosia main road, which enabled them to increase the rate of reinforcements and equipment arriving from Turkey, something essential for the second planned offensive. During the cease fire they expanded east and west controlling 7% of the island.

Chapter 14
The 23rd July 1974

Turkish Air Force Jet Nicosia Airport low attack

Nicosia

06.00 hours Turkish Forces attempted to advance south to Nicosia International Airport boundaries.

At 07.00 hours Greek Cypriot National Guard 35th Commando were transported to the airport to join the Greek Regiment (ELDYK), Greek Cypriot National Guard and airport paramilitary police, the latter were equipped with anti-tank weapons and five M8 Greyhound armoured vehicles, to defend it from an anticipated attack by Turkish Forces moving through the Kyrenia-Nicosia bridgehead

They arrived just in time to mount a defence. They assumed fighting positions in and around the main terminal building and selected key locations.

A convoy of Turkish vehicles arrived at the north end of the airport, about five hundred metres from the defenders. The main plan of the defenders, was deploying a number of machine guns and anti-tank weapons, three 90mm, EM69s and allow the Turkish Forces to advance into the path of their fire. The Turkish Forces advance units spotted some of the enemy positions, changed their tactics and commenced a general forward attack from the north.

The initial wave of around a company of Turkish Infantry attack was blunted by heavy weapons and small arms fire from the Greek Cypriot National Guard positions to the south, with the Greek Cypriot National Guard and the Greek Regiment (ELDYK) opening fire from the terminal building on the flank. Conceding defeat, the Turkish Forces fell back to their original positions with significant casualties. They then regrouped and advanced again, this time in battalion strength towards the positions of the Greek Cypriot National Guard, braving a withering hail of bullets. In turn, the Turkish Forces commenced fire from their rear-line with a 4.2-inch (110mm) mortar from the direction of the adjacent United Nations Camp UNFICYP. The Greek Cypriot National Guard now launched a counter-attack against the Turkish Infantry within the airport perimeter by assaulting the ground troops with their five M8 Greyhound armoured vehicles.

The Turkish Forces sited beside the United Nations Camp UNFICYP were targeted by the Greek Cypriot National Guard, who fired M-79 phosphorus grenades at them in order to cause a bush fire and smoke. A 90mm anti-tank rocket was also fired in the direction of a suspected Turkish observation post in a house on the northern edge of the airport, forcing it to be abandoned. Two Turkish M-47 tanks of the 39th Divisional Tank Battalion, attempted a diversionary attack to the eastern side of the airport terminal building.

They were subsequently destroyed by Greek Cypriot National Guard with M-20 Super Bazookas.

As darkness approached, after hours of fierce battle, both the Greek Cypriot National Guard and Turkish Forces began to cease operations, with Turkish Forces gaining no advancement.

Under the ceasefire agreement both sides were informed, it was agreed that the United Nations should take full control of the airport while each side would evacuate the new protected area and would remain at least 50 metres from the perimeter of the airport. The Turkish Forces then vacated the airport retreating back north to their original positions. The Greek Cypriot National Guard and Greek Regiment (ELDYK) then vacated the Airport Buildings and all the surrounding areas. The estimated size of the Greek Cypriot National Guard and the Greek Regiment (ELDYK) was clear to see as they vacated the airport.

Two T-34 medium tanks, eight armoured cars, three armoured personnel carriers, five 100m field guns, five vehicles mounted with heavy quadruple machine guns, five Bofors anti-aircraft guns, five jeep mounted 105mm anti-tank guns, five trucks of ammunition and six busloads of troops.

This formidable force would have vigorously defended the airport resulting in a huge loss of life on both sides and massive damage to the infrastructure of the terminal building and airport complex. That evening, United Nations Personnel placed further obstacles along the runways and a UN flag was flown from the roof of the terminal building. Due to a shortage of suitable armoured cars, airport fire trucks were used as patrol vehicles.

The United Nations Force had taken over territory in order to achieve peace and prevent more killings and bloodshed. Though subsequent events would demonstrate the peace was not as solid as it appeared. With the ceasefire established, HQ UNFICYP faced the challenge of holding the airport. The airport fell within the jurisdiction of the Canadian sector (CANCON), however, the past days had drained the strength from Canada's reserves as they re-established and guarded United Nations posts on the Nicosia Green Line, including the Ledra Palace Hotel, where fierce fighting was taking place.

During the day Nikos Sampson resigned, turning over the presidency to Glafkos Clerides, a respected Greek Cypriot leader who as House speaker, was also Makarios's constitutional successor. A general ceasefire was declared, but in many parts of the island, this was not adhered to. The capture of Nicosia International Airport was one of the few main objectives that the Turkish Forces decisively failed to achieve during the intervention.

Kyrenia

At 11.00 hours The Turkish Forces from their advantageous firing positions at Bellapais attacked and encircled the Greek Cypriot National Guard 191st POP Artillery Company and 181st Artillery Battalion. The Greek Cypriot National Guard 181st Artillery Battalion lost four 12.7mm artillery guns along with twelve 25 pounder artillery guns. The 191st POP Artillery Company lost three 75mm artillery guns. The entire 181st Artillery Battalion refused to surrender, resulting in its annihilation with the loss of all its personnel.

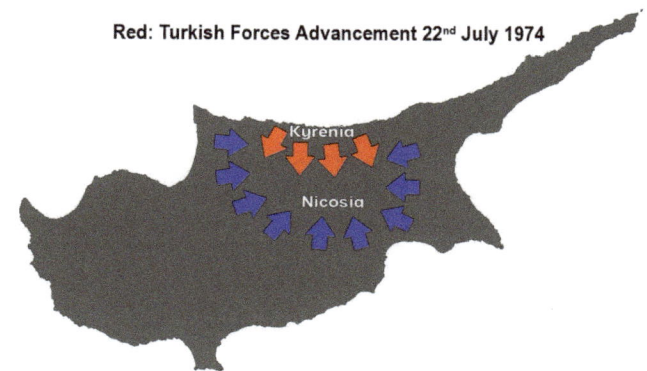

Red: Turkish Forces Advancement 22nd July 1974

Blue: Greek Cypriot National Guard Defences 22nd July 1974

Chapter 15
My Involvement In Nicosia International Airport

Operations Brief the 23rd of July 1974

The force Commander stated to the International media that all United Nations nationalities were deployed in the airport. After the afternoon operations brief on the 23rd of July 1974 at 15.00 hours, the Force Commander asked me if there was any communication from Commandant J. Flynn, I replied *"no sir, I have tried to make contact with him on six occasions today"*. He then remarked that no Irish troops were deployed in the Airport despite the fact he had stated to the International media that all United Nation nationalities were deployed there and were in full control of the airport.

Force Commander Brigadier General D. Prem Chand in discussion with Sgt Jim Casey Chief Clerk Operations Branch prior to his departure to join the United Nations forces in the Airport.

He asked would I have any problem going to the terminal in the Airport to join the other nationalities there. Without time to think I replied, "*sir it would be an honour to do so*". He replied jokingly with only three Irish troops serving at UNFICYP, you will be representing your country and it will be an honour for you to do so! Arrangements were made through HQ Britcon to issue me with equipment and transport to the airport terminal building.

Personal Weapon

I had no personal weapon as we brought none to Cyprus it would not have been possible as we flew commercial airlines. I went to the British Armoury store on instructions from the British Regimental Sgt Major WO1 Mr. Birch to be issued with a weapon and UN helmet. After a brief introduction to the operations of a Sten gun, I was issued with same and a large supply of ammunition. It is similar to our own Gustaf. "*Just imagine the British Army issuing an Irishman a Sten gun*".

Drop-off at Nicosia International Airport

At 17.00 hours I was taken in a United Nations British ferret scout car to the main entrance of the Airport terminal. I emerged from AFV and ran into the terminal building, heavy small arms and machine gun fire was being directed at the terminal building by Turkish Forces at the time.

Situation on Arrival

I was welcomed by a Canadian Major, if I recall correctly, his name was Major Harries he thought it very amusing that I was selected as an individual to join the United Nations Forces in the Airport and he introduced me to a number of Canadian soldiers and instructed me to remain with them at all times and carry out any actions as instructed.

I was horrified with what I saw on entering the Airport the floors were covered in blood and it also ran down the walls and stairs and the stench was unbearable, a Canadian Warrant Officer Roy McKay whom I befriended, informed me that the bodies of Greek Cypriot National Guard Soldiers and Greek Cypriot Tactical Reserve Corps (Greek Cypriot Policemen) were removed to a hangar just outside the building. The remains of a British Airways Trident Jet bombed by Turkish Air force lay in a heap on the main runway with other commercial and private aircraft also badly damaged.

Remains of Cyprus Airways Trident Jet

The runway was cratered in numerous locations rendering it unusable. Most of the windows and doors in the building were blasted out but, in my opinion, the Turkish Forces wanted to take the main terminal building intact. The gorse around the airport was also burning with smoke causing eyes to water. As the heat of the day subsided and darkness fell with a light breeze the stench was unbearable. I am led to believe the stench was caused by a number of bodies of Turkish Paratroopers in the adjacent fields. They were killed after landing on the open plain and during the fire fights with the Greek Cypriot National Guard soldiers and Greek Regiment (ELDYK) defending the airport and snipers from the Grammar School just outside the perimeter north-east of the Airport.

I was informed by Canadian Sgt Major Roy McKay that we were severely undermanned and under-strength. He said there was an infantry platoon in the airport, plus clerks, mechanics, drivers, and cooks of United Nations Personnel. They had managed to find men who could operate sub-machine guns and 106 mm anti-tank guns. If the Turkish Forces attacked, we would not have fire power supremacy, to take them on. He said that the guys were ready to remain in position to fight to the end. They were ready to fight if the perimeter of the airport was violated by the Turkish Forces. The Airport at all costs, must be held, despite the fact that an entire Turkish Battalion was 500 meters north of us on the Morphou Road. As a show of strength he said, his Canadian soldiers and the other nationalities would spend the entire night and to-morrow night outside on the runway. He then said I can assure you we won't be short of the best of food, all the airport catering food in the refrigerators will have to be used as it will thaw out due to lack of electricity.

On the Turkish mainland, the failure to capture the Nicosia Airport was likely hidden from government officials because of ongoing communication problems. Radio Ankara reported on 24th of July that Turkish Forces held the Airport. The Turkish Vice President's Office also began issuing threats and statements stating that Turkish Forces should not be denied access to the airport as they already held de-facto control over it before the United Nations took it over. This was untrue, it was held by Greek Cypriot National Guard and Greek Regiment (ELDYK) prior to the takeover.

Journalists at Nicosia International Airport

To clarify the situation and ease tensions, HQ UNFICYP Force Commander Brigadier General Prem Chand brought journalists to Nicosia Airport to show that the United Nations held it to the exclusion of all others. However, Turkish tanks continued to move closer to the airfield entering through the perimeter fence. This indicated a major chain-of-command problem between the Turkish military and Turkish government officials. I spoke briefly with a journalist who introduced himself as Alan Bestic and he asked if I would talk to him at another suitable time. Another journalist asked me why there were only three Irish soldiers serving in Cyprus, I replied *"we can easily do the work of 300 soldiers"*, he was not amused with my reply, but no time for any more discussions as I could see by their reaction to the approach of the Turkish tanks, they could not wait to high tail it out of the Airport.

Greek Cypriot National Guard plus ELDYK and Turkish Forces

Shortly after the journalists departed the Turkish tanks opened up firing, backed by machine guns on the Greek Cypriot National Guard positions to the South of their position, this was returned with mortar fire and heavy machine gun fire by the Cypriot National Guard. Quite a number of shells hit the runway very close to the terminal building. We had at this stage taken defensive positions within the buildings.

It was then learned that the Turkish government had issued an ultimatum and intended to seize the airport during the night. Clearly that put the United Nations in an intolerable position and they would have to defend the airport at all costs. The British Government was also alarmed by this threat and offered reinforcements to HQ UNFICYP, this was immediately accepted by HQ United Nations New York.

Order Restored

At 16.00 hours on the 25th of July 1974 order was restored in the airport and all seemed normal. The Turkish Battalion had retreated north into the enclave and the Greek Cypriot National Guard moved from the southern perimeter of the airport with HQ UNFICYP in full control of the Airport and all roads leading to it. On the morning of the 26th of July 1974 at approximately 07.30 hours I was relieved by CQMS Tony Byrne and a

Canadian Officer authorised the handover. I then returned to Headquarters in a British AFV and resumed my role as Chief Clerk Operations Branch. In November 1974 we eventually left Cyprus from a British Base to Beirut then on to Ireland. It was a tour of duty that will remain in my mind forever. I served three more tours of duty in Cyprus prior to my retirement in 1986.

Chapter 16
The 24th July to 14th August

Reinforcements Nicosia International Airport

After agreement with United Nations Headquarters, United Kingdom authorized the deployment of 12 RAF Phantom jets to Cyprus. They arrived at 05.00 hours on 25th of July. British armoured reconnaissance reinforcements from British Sovereign bases areas arrived at 08.00 hours on the 24th of July 1974, as additions to HQ UNFICYP.

The 16th/5th Queen's Royal Lancers, co-opted to United Nations Force, provided the strength, equipment and weaponry that had been lacking by United Nations soldiers the previous night, and their arrival marked the turning point for the airport crisis. The 4th/7th Dragoon Guards and 2nd Battalion of Coldstream Guards also co-opted to United Nations Force, concentrated the defence of the terminal building. The stronger forces meant that Turkish Forces no longer faced a lightly armed United Nations Force but was confronted by the weight of a well-equipped military force, they were informed of the new reinforcements. The Turkish threat subsided immediately in the face of this newfound strength.

Incidents during the period

Saint Ermolaos

A village in the Kyrenia district. In 1974 the population was five hundred and six Greek Cypriots. They were all forced to leave their homes by advancing Turkish Forces and fled south for the safety of their lives. Displaced Turkish

Cypriots from the south of the island and Turkish citizens from mainland Turkey subsequently moved to this village and it was named Şirinevler in Turkish in 1975.

Sysklipos
Situated in the Kyrenia District, on the southern slopes of the western part of the Five Finger mountains. In 1974 the population was two hundred and fifty-six Greek Cypriots. They were all forced to leave their homes by advancing Turkish Forces and fled south for the safety of their lives. A total of twenty-seven Greek Cypriots were missing after the evacuation of the village and are unaccountable for. Today the village is barely habitable with ninety-five displaced Turkish Cypriots from the south living there.

The 26th of July
The villages of Saint Ermolaos and Sisklipos, as well as the pass of Saint Pavlos, the Greek Cypriots fled for their safety and lives before the Turkish Forces advancement. Turkish Forces occupied and took over the village. Displaced Turkish Cypriots from the south of the island and Turkish citizens from mainland Turkey subsequently moved to this village and it was named Şirinevler in Turkish in 1975.

The 27th of July
The village of Saint Ermolaos was attacked and recaptured by Greek Cypriot National Guard, forcing Turkish Forces to retreat from the village.

The 28th of July
Turkish Forces re-attacked the village of Saint Ermolaos, after a sustained Turkish Forces assault the Greek Cypriot National Guard were forced to retreat.

Karavas

A village in the north of Cyprus. In 1974 it had a Greek Cypriot population of approximately four thousand. They were all forced to leave their homes by advancing Turkish Forces and fled south for the safety of their lives. Following the population exchange assisted by the United Nations where the Turkish Cypriots forced from their villages in the South were transported to the safety of the North, today the village is home to Turkish Cypriots displaced from their original village Mandria in Paphos.

The 1st of August

Heavy fighting commenced at Karavas with the Turkish Forces 28th Division attacking and removing Greek Cypriot National Guard 316th Battalion from Kornos hill 1024 in the western Kyrenia mountains. During the night B Company of Greek Cypriot National Guard 31-MK Commandos assaulted hill 1024 and re took it from the Turkish Forces. One Turkish M-47 tank from 28th Divisional Tank Battalion was reported destroyed by a 3-M-6 Shell anti-tank missile fired by Greek Cypriot National Guard.

Turkish M-47 Tank captured by Greek Cypriot National Guard

The 2nd of August

Early morning the Turkish Forces re-attacked Kornos hill 1024, but failed to re-capture it due to heavy resistance by B Company Greek Cypriot

National Guard 31-MK Commandos and they withdrew. In the afternoon a second major attack with a larger Turkish Force of the 28th Division was mounted successfully, forcing the Greek Cypriot National Guard to retreat. During the retreat the Greek Cypriot National Guard 316th Battalion who originally held the hill on the 1st of August laid an ambush against the Turkish Forces, destroying a M-47 tank and an M-113. They then captured a M-47tank from 28th Divisional Tank Regiment, (the T-47 tank was later used against the Turkish Forces by Greek Cypriot National Guard during a tank battle in Skylloura, confusing the Turkish Forces as it still retained its Turkish markings). In addition they destroyed one M-113 armoured personnel carrier of 230th Mechanised Infantry Regiment and captured another M-113. They failed to retake the hill, then retreated south.

The 3rd of August
The Greek Cypriot National Guard 316th, 321st and 256th Infantry Battalions, as well as a company of irregulars and the Greek Regiment (ELDYK) established a defensive line on the western front from Karavas to Lapithos corridor. This was to blockade use of the corridor by the Turkish Forces.

The 3rd of August
Village of Sysklipos - It was reported that in the village of Sysklipos fourteen Greek Cypriots were killed in a house and their bodies buried in a mass grave by Turkish Forces. Those who remained in the village disappeared on the 26th of August, they are still missing.

The 6th of August
Early dawn, two divisions of the Turkish Forces 28th Division and 61st Infantry Regiment attacked the Greek Cypriot National Guard 256th Infantry Battalion and Greek Regiment (ELDYK) defensive line at the village of Vassilia, Kyrenia with heavy artillery and mortar fire supported by naval artillery.

The Turkish Forces were gaining ground west to Karavas and north east to Lapithos. With combined artillery cover, tanks, and marine forces, the Turkish 28th Division extended west into Karavas, while a Turkish Commando Brigade and the Turkish 61st Infantry Regiment moved over the Pentedaktylos mountains to flank the Greek Cypriot National Guard from the north-east.

The Turkish Air Force extensively bombed the areas of Laipthos-Karavas to Vavila-Vassilia during this offensive. The battle continued fiercely with Turkish Forces gaining more ground. The Greek Regiment (ELDYK) attacked elements of the Turkish 61st Regiment with mortars. During the battle, two Turkish M-47 tanks were engaged with recoilless rifles and destroyed. In the afternoon, all Greek Cypriot forces in the area retreated to the Vasilia-Vavila defensive line.

The 7th of August
The Turkish Forces 28th Division attacked the Vasilia-Vavila defensive line with supportive artillery fire, but no infantry attack was made.

The 8th of August

Lapithos Town

Lapithos is a town on the northern coast of Cyprus. In 1974 it had a population of three thousand one hundred and sixteen Greek Cypriots plus six others. They were forced to leave their homes with the advance of the Turkish Forces and fled south for the safety of their lives.

Turkish Forces advancing

Turkish Forces occupy Lapithos after two days of resistance there by Greek Cypriot National Guard. Ninety-one Greek Cypriots were reported missing or killed and forty taken as prisoners of war. From this point on there were a number of fire fights between Turkish Forces 28th Division and the Greek Cypriot National Guard 256th Battalion with huge casualties on both sides and Turkish Forces secretly gaining ground east and west all the time.

Turkish Forces preparing an assault

Chapter 17

The 14th August Renewal of Turkish Offensive

Attila II

Turkish Forces, reinforced to the strength of two infantry divisions and supporting elements, commenced a second major offensive, codenamed Attila II. This offensive lasted three days and caused the defences of the Greek Cypriot National Guard and the Greek regiment (ELDYK) to collapse, leading to the capture of the towns of Famagusta, Morphou, and the northern quarter of Nicosia. The Greek Cypriots attempted to mount their main eastern defensive line between Mia Millia and Nea Chorio villages, northeast of Nicosia, without success.

Then early morning on the 14th of August 1974, Turkey violated the ceasefire agreement signed on the 23rd of July 1974 by massing a ground force, mortar, artillery and air strike assaults on all sides. Attempting to gain ground, the breakout to the west was spearheaded by the Turkish 28th Divisions and the Commando Brigade, heading for Morphou and Kormakiti. It easily brushed aside the Greek Cypriot National Guard and Greek Regiment (ELDYK) defenders of the 231st and 281st Battalions, pushing them back to their final "Troodos Line" to the south. To the east, the Turkish 39th Division's tanks and armoured personnel carriers attacked along two axes, one raced east towards Famagusta and another to the south east towards Mia Milia, and on towards Larnaca. The Greek Cypriot National Guard, Greek Regiment

(ELDYK) defenders and twenty-four T-34 medium tanks defending the eastern sector were quite simply overwhelmed and withdrew south. The Turkish objective was to gain control of a central line stretching across the island from Famagusta on the east to the Bay of Morphou on the west. They already held the area from Kyrenia to north Nicosia.

The Turkish Forces advanced beyond their previously observed United Nations ceasefire lines and engaged in three days of assault against the Greek Cypriot National Guard and Greek Regiment (ELDYK). To the east Morphou and Lefka both fell to Turkish Forces. Each axis comprised of tanks, infantry assault artillery and aircraft bombardments this attack was the most aggressive one of the conflict.

Greek Cypriot National Guard were left scrambling in the face of the advancing Turkish Forces and offered little resistance. The westward Turkish offensive put them once again into striking distance of the Nicosia International Airport. This time, rather than risk another standoff at the airport, the Turkish Forces sought to encircle the airport, capture a key road junction leading to the airport, and effectively cut off the United Nations defenders. This strategy led to the most protracted fighting between the Cypriot National Guard and Turkish Forces during the second phase.

At 10.30 hours the Greek Cypriot National Guard defence lines at Mia Milia, defended by 173rd Anti-tank Battalion, supporting 399th Infantry Battalion were attacked and over-run by the Turkish Forces. This resulted in an urgent retreat, in the process nine artillery 6 pounder guns were left at their firing positions.

Amid the fighting, United Nations Camps were again stranded in the direct line of fire and were heavily shelled. Throughout the island, the second phase of the conflict brought UNFICYP Forces deeper into the conflict around them. Warnings were given to both the Cypriot National Guard and Turkish Forces to stop firing on United Nations property, vehicles, and personnel.

On the 14th of August 1974, at Boghazi, the Boghazi Squadron of the Cypriot Navy scuttled three motor torpedo boats P-4 Skinheads and one patrol boat R -151 to prevent Turkish Forces from making use of them.

The situation worsened when Greek Cypriot National Guard and Turkish Forces began putting United Nations markings on their vehicles to get around roadblocks. The result was a complete disregard for the United Nations banner which, in turn, led to shots being fired at anyone carrying binoculars, maps or radios.

This confusion proved to be fatal for three unfortunate Austrian United Nations soldiers in a United Nations jeep, clearly marked and with UN signs and a flag flying. It was bombed and incinerated with napalm by a Turkish fighter jet on the 14th of August 1974 on the old Nicosia/Larnaca Road. The United Nations banner no longer provided protection or safety for the UNFICYP Forces.

Remains of Three Austrian Soldiers

The Battle of Agios Dometios Nicosia

The 336th Greek Cypriot National Guard Reserve Battalion was in charge of defending the area between Ledra Palace in Nicosia and the (ELDYK) military camp near the Grammar School close to Nicosia airport, encompassing around 3.5 kilometres. Three hundred and twenty (ELDYK) soldiers were in charge of defending their camp and the area around it. The Grammar school was being used as a forward command post by Greek Cypriot National Guard and Greek Regiment (ELDYK).

At approximately 05.00 hours on the 14th of August 1974, the Turkish Air Force bombarded Greek Cypriot National Guard targets alongside the (ELDYK) camp and Grammar School in Ayios Dhometrios Nicosia and additional shelling by Turkish artillery on the area close to Nicosia International Airport. Followed by approximately seven hundred Turkish troops attempting to move in on the ELDYK camp. They were met with strong resistance, casualties and failed to achieve their objective.

On the 15th of August 1974, a number of M-47/48 tanks arrived with troop reinforcements, it was estimated to be in the region of two thousand plus to assist the Turkish Forces already engaged. Fierce fighting took place all day, with air strikes on the Greek Regiment (ELDYK) camp and Grammar School.

An unknown Greek Cypriot National Guard forward observation post managed to call in artillery fire on the advancing Turkish Forces from widely dispersed batteries of different guns. This artillery bombardment was deadly accurate and separated the Turkish armour from the infantry, causing serious casualties until a napalm airstrike located and silenced the forward observation post. Again the Turkish Forces were met with very strong resistance and failed to capture the Grammar School or ELDYK Camp.

On the morning of the 16th of August, a vicious battle took place between the Turkish Forces, the ELDYK camp and the Grammar School. After the area had been softened up by continuous bombing and napalm attacks, leaving the Grammar School collapsed in the centre. In the region of two thousand Turkish soldiers of the reinforced joined the Turkish Forces already there, supported by seventeen M-47/48 tanks, assaulted the ELDYK Camp and Grammar School.

Again, the Turkish Forces were met with very strong resistance and gaining little ground. Due to the lack of reinforcements, artillery/mortar support, food, water and depletion of ammunition the Greek Regiment (ELDYK) and Greek Cypriot National Guard surrendered, with the Turkish Forces taking control of the camp and Grammar School. Both sides fought hard and brave in this battle, but credit must be given to the defenders for their bravery by holding out for three days against the huge odds they faced. During the battle it is alleged that Greek Cypriot National Guard and Greek Regiment (ELDYK) has over eighty-three causalities. The Turkish Forces lost five M-47/48 tanks, four were destroyed by light anti-tank weapons and the fifth by an artillery strike, they also suffered an unknown number of deaths and casualties.

After taking the ELDYK Camp and Grammar School The Turkish Regiment, attempted to re-encircle Nicosia International Airport they were met with fierce resistance from the Greek Cypriot National Guard 212th Infantry Battalion and "A" Raider Squadron. Their attempt was unsuccessful and they retreated back to the area of the Grammar School.

The Turkish Forces also tried breaking through the defensive lines and fighting very hard to take the Imprisoned Graves, using all available air power, land assets and Turkish infantry, they used narrow roads to try and outflank Greek Cypriot National Guard units, they were unsuccessful in all their attempts due to heavy resistance. They lost one M-47 that afternoon when destroyed by strikes from a Greek Cypriot National Guard T-34 medium tank.

The Turkish assault on the Greek Regiment (ELDYK) camp and Grammar School was eventually successful, but the Greek Cypriot National Guard and Greek Regiment (ELDYK) successfully defended most of Ayios Dhometrios and Agios Pavlos areas, thus preventing key areas such as the Imprisoned Graves, from falling into the Turkish hands. At 1800 hours the National Flag of Turkey was hoisted on the roof of the Grammar School.

Artillery bombardment on Turkish Forces at (ELDYK) camp and Grammar School by Greek Cypriot National Guard artillery.

The 14th of August Greek Cypriot National Guard Eastern Sector Defences

At 06.30 hours, on the Eastern sector, the Turkish Navy, Air Force and Artillery began firing at the Greek Cypriot National Guard positions. The Greek Cypriot National Guard counter-artillery fire was no match to silence the superior Turkish fire.

Turkish units of the 39th Division attacked the Mia Milia defensive line of the Greek Cypriot National Guard. The line was held by the Greek-Cypriot National Guard 399th Infantry Battalion reinforced with two 3-M-6 Shmel missile launchers, four 106mm recoilless rifles and twelve 6-pounder anti-tank guns. The 399th Infantry Battalion used a small dried-out river bed as an anti-tank ditch, and laid anti-tank mines in front of the ditch. The United Nations were informed where the clear roads through the minefields were, and possibly the Turkish 39th Division knew of them too. The initial Turkish Forces attacked with infantry against Koutsoventis and Mia Milia locations were repelled. They were swiftly followed by armoured attacks. The Turkish tanks circumnavigated the Greek Cypriot National Guard minefields at Mia Milia. At 10.00 hours they reached the Greek Cypriot National Guard lines of 399th Infantry Battalion and at 10.30 hours they had broken through, cutting the 399th Infantry Battalion in two. At 10.55 hours the GEEF (High Command of the Cypriot National Guard) ordered the Eastern Sector Command to withdraw to the Troodos line. The 241st Infantry Battalion acting as the reserve of the 12th Tactical Group delayed the Turkish Forces until 11.00 hours, but lacking anti-tank weapons it started withdrawing immediately towards Famagusta.

Following the collapse of the Greek Cypriot National Guard defensive line, the GEEF ordered the 226th Infantry Battalion to mount a defensive line together with the 341st Reserve Battalion in order to delay the Turkish Forces. The 226th Infantry Battalion retreated at 18.00 hours to the south, while the 341st stayed put. The Turkish Air Force started bombing the retreating Greek Cypriot National Guard and the Greek-Cypriot Artillery Battalions started retreating to the east as well. The 9th Tactical Group, even though it had not been attacked, faced the danger of encirclement from the south and so started its retreat by 12.00 hours towards Famagusta.

In the western sector, the hilltop Aspros, which had been used as an observation post, was abandoned by Greek-Cypriot National Guard after a Turkish Forces attack. No effort to recapture it was made.

The 14th of August - Famagusta

Famagusta, a historically significant port city located on the eastern coast of

Cyprus, held immense economic and strategic value. Its deep-sea harbour and tourism industry contributed significantly to the island's economy. In the early 1970s, Famagusta was the number-one tourist destination in Cyprus. To cater to the increasing number of tourists, many new high-rise buildings and hotels were constructed. During its heyday, Varosha was not only the number-one tourist destination in Cyprus, but between 1970 and 1974, it was one of the most popular tourist destinations in the world and was a favourite destination for such celebrities as Elizabeth Taylor, Richard Burton, Raquel Welch, and Brigitte Bardot.

Varosha Famagusta prior to 1974

Famagusta City

Control over Famagusta became a crucial objective for both Greek Cypriot and Turkish Forces during the conflict.

The Greek Cypriot National Guard in Famagusta, were determined to defend the city against the advancing Turkish Forces. They established defensive positions, erected barricades, and utilized artillery and other weaponry to protect the city and its inhabitants.

Turkish Forces subjected Famagusta to intense bombardment and aerial attacks. The city was surrounded, cutting off supplies and communication. The Turkish military employed heavy artillery, mortars, and sophisticated weaponry, including naval and air bombardment, to weaken the Greek Cypriot National Guard 341st Infantry Battalion defences.

Despite the relentless Turkish assault, Greek Cypriot National Guard displayed remarkable resilience and courage. They fiercely defended the city and effectively repelled Turkish attempts to infiltrate their positions from the 14th to the 16th of August 1974, leading to a stalemate situation.

With dwindling supplies, mounting casualties, and the increasing risk to civilians, Greek Cypriot leaders in Famagusta eventually chose to surrender the city at 17.00 hours on the 16th of August 1974, with Greek Cypriot National Guard withdrawing to Larnaca. One Turkish M-47 tank was reported destroyed by M-40-A1 recoilless rifle fire. Three Greek Cypriot National Guard T-34 medium tanks were abandoned plus six artillery 6 pounder guns.

Turkish Forces occupied Famagusta, and the city fell under Turkish control, beginning a new chapter in its history.

The Greek Cypriot population, estimated to be around 40,000, fled the city, seeking refuge in the south. The sudden displacement and loss of their homes had a profound impact on the lives of the people of Famagusta.

Today, Famagusta stands as a ghost town, its once-thriving streets and buildings abandoned and dilapidated. The battle serves as a powerful symbol of the wider conflicts in Cyprus, representing the devastating consequences of war.

Not all of Famagusta is abandoned. There's still a large section of the city itself which is still very much inhabited and active by Turkish Nationals and Turkish Cypriots. A section of Famagusta, known as Varosha, is essentially abandoned. Prior to 1974, Varosha was among the most sought-after tourist destinations in the world, flaunting its luxurious hotels and golden beaches. But the landscape changed dramatically with the Turkish intervention. As the Turkish Troops advanced, Varosha's residents fled their homes, fearing for their lives, hoping to return once the dust of conflict settled. But that return never materialised. The Turkish military took complete control of Varosha, fencing it off from the outside world, by land and sea and prohibiting entry to the area.

Ghost town Varosha Famagusta

This former tourist haven has since transformed into a ghost town. Over time, the hotels and homes began to crumble, and nature started weaving its way back through the abandoned urban spaces. The eeriness of empty beaches juxtaposed with decaying high-rise buildings has made Varosha a haunting emblem of the Cyprus conflict.

The 14th of August - Villages of Maratha, Santalaris and Aloda

It was reported that in the villages of Maratha and Santalaris, eighty-eight Turkish Cypriots were killed by Greek Cypriot gunmen (possible EOKA B). Elderly people and children were also killed during the massacre; it was reported that only six people survived. In the village of Aloda thirty-eight Turkish Cypriots were also massacred by the same Greek Cypriot gunmen, only three escaped the massacre.

The bodies of one hundred and twenty six of the three villages were buried in a mass grave with the aid of a bulldozer. Parts of the bodies had been chopped off with sharp tools, machine guns had also been used in the massacre. The United Nations described the massacre as a crime against humanity, by saying "constituting a further crime against humanity committed by the Greek and Greek Cypriot gunmen."

The 14th of August - The Villages of Tochni and Zyggi

It was reported that EOKA-B gunmen rounded up all the men and boys from the villages of Tochni and Zyggi a total of eighty-five and held them hostage in a primary school overnight. Next morning, all the men and boys were forced onto a bus. They were told they would be taken to a prison camp, just like the thousands of other Turkish Cypriot men on the island.

The bus instead took the eighty-five to the village of Palodia where they were lined up and gunned down by machine guns. Only one person survived and escaped. Bulldozers were later used to create a makeshift mass grave to hide the bodies before Turkish Forces or United Nations could discover them. Later that month, the remaining Turkish Cypriot residents were evacuated using United Nations military vehicles. The evacuation was carried out by

7th Squadron Royal Corp of Transport (RCT) who were serving with the United Nations at Camp UNFICYP Nicosia.

The 15th of August - Tank Battle

Tank Battle

Turkish Forces and Greek Cypriot National Guard tanks encounter each other in the only known tank-to-tank battle of the conflict.

The Turkish Forces attack in the western area started early morning, with mortar fire at the Greek Cypriot National Guard positions in the village of Skylloura, between Morphou and Nicosia. At 13.30 hours a company of thirteen M-47 tanks were observed approaching the village of Skylloura, of which three moved towards the village of Agios Vassilios.

A Turkish M-47 tank previously captured by Greek Cypriot National Guard on the 2nd of August 1974, manned by them and still bearing Turkish markings was located in the village. The Greek Cypriot National Guard had three T-34 medium tanks concealed in a football stadium in the village. As the ten Turkish M-47 tanks entered the village, the Turkish captured M -47 tank passed them as it left the village. The Turkish Forces mistakenly took it for one of their own tanks. Outside the village the three M-47 tanks that had previously headed for Agios Vassilios were seen approaching a bridge. The M-47 tank manned by the three Greek Cypriot National Guard and two ELDYK soldiers opened fire on the M-47 tanks with the assistance of their T-34 medium tanks. They then opened fire on the ten M-47 tanks in the village. After causing considerable damage to seven of the Turkish M-47 tanks and one completely destroyed, the Turkish Forces eventually realized that the M-47 tank was their enemy and then opened fire on it, striking and damaging it with a 90mm projectile, but the occupants of the tank survived. The Turkish M-47 tanks were forced to retreat to safety due to heavy artillery fire directed at them by the Greek Cypriot National Guard 183rd Artillery Battalion.

The 15th of August Greek Cypriot National Guard Defence Lines

On the eastern sector, the retreating units of the Greek-Cypriot 12th Tactical Group crossed the defence line of the 341st Infantry Battalion at 10.30 hours. The 341st Reserve Battalion reinforced with three T-34 tanks and six 6-pounder guns was isolated and holding the defence line west of Famagusta on its own. The remainder of Greek Cypriot National Guard units continued their retreat to Larnaca and the Troodos main defence line.

At 14.00 hours the Greek-Cypriot National Guard 341st Infantry Battalion observed the Turkish tanks and the Turkish Forces 14th Infantry Regiment approaching. Realizing it was abandoned and isolated, the command of the 341st Infantry Battalion ordered retreat at 17.00 hours, covered by their T-34 tanks. The T-34 tanks (immobilized due to mechanical failures) and the six 6-pounder guns were left behind at their positions.

The first Turkish Forces units, including four M-47 tanks and eleven M-113 APCs, entered the Turkish Cypriot enclave of Famagusta at 17.30 hours. They united with the Turkish-Cypriot units, but did not enter the undefended Greek-Cypriot district.

The central sector saw a heavy exchange of fire, but no major engagements took place.

In the western sector, the armoured units of the Turkish Forces 28th Division made contact with the Greek Cypriot National Guard at about 14.30 hours. The 28th Division's attack was augmented by the Turkish Commando Brigade's advance to the east. In total the Turkish units advanced up to six kilometres to the west. On the night of the 15th and 16th of August, the Greek-Cypriot National Guard 11th Tactical Group (responsible for the western sector) was ordered to withdraw to the Troodos defence line.

The 15th – 16th of August - Villages of Murataga, Sandallar and Atlilar

It was reported that eighty-nine Turkish Cypriots were massacred in the villages of Murataga and Sandallar. A further thirty-seven Turkish Cypriots from the village of Atlilar were also murdered by Greek Cypriot fighters (possibly EOKA B fighters). One hundred and twenty-six Turkish Cypriot men, women and children were slaughtered in total.

The 16th of August Greek Cypriot National Guard Sectors

In the eastern sector, Turkish Forces consolidated their gains but made no major actions. Greek Cypriot National Guard reorganized for defence on the Troodos line. The Turkish Forces continued southwards and pushed back the Greek Cypriot National Guard 212th Infantry Battalion. It stopped after receiving return fire from Greek Cypriot National Guard anti-tank fire. They also attacked the 336th Infantry Battalion inside Nicosia, advancing one hundred metres, but received fifty casualties. Tactical Group had retreated to the Troodos line. Two platoons were left to keep contact with the advancing Turkish Forces. The Turkish Forces advanced slowly to the east, Morphou was captured at 12.30 hours and Limnitis at 18.00 hours. Despite a cease fire in the western sector the Turkish Forces had not yet assaulted the Troodos line. As a result, on the 17th of August 1974 both the Greek Cypriot National Guard and the Turkish High Commands ordered their units to advance. Several Greek-Cypriot units in the western sector suffered badly from desertions, as poorly disciplined reservists abandoned their units. The Troodos line was thus poorly manned.

The 16th of August - Prastio Famagusta

It was reported that Turkish Forces took eight Greek Cypriots prisoner and later executed them. Turkish Forces advanced south, east and west now occupying, 37% of the island which is under Turkish control.

The 16th and 17th of August - Pyroi and Louroujina

On the 16th and 17th of August 1974 the final battle took place at Pyroi village, just north of Louroujina village. It had a mixed population of three hundred and seventy-four Greek Cypriots and eighty-six Turkish Cypriots. Turkish Forces advanced south towards Pyroi village. A Greek Cypriot National Guard platoon with T-34 tank support attempted to repel the Turkish Infantry Battalion entering the village.

The Turkish Forces laid down an artillery barrage in advance of their troops. After several hours of battle, the Greek Cypriot National Guard were no match for the Turkish Forces, they retreated south from the village towards

Larnaca along with the Greek Cypriot residents. One T-34 tank was immobilized when struck by Turkish anti-tank fire and four T-34s tanks abandoned on the road as they fled, these were later captured by Turkish Forces. The Turkish Forces entered the village, taking control and then advanced south to the Turkish Cypriot village of Lourourina thus creating what became known as "the Louroujina bubble". They also held control of the Nicosia to Larnaca road. Louroujina was the deepest incursion into Greek Cypriot territory the Turkish Forces managed to secure. The reason for this incursion as claimed by the Turkish Forces, Louroujina had a population of one thousand nine hundred and sixty-three Turkish Cypriots in the enclave. There were concerns that a massacre might occur, if the village was not secured. At Stake for the Greek Cypriots was control of the Nicosia / Larnaca road. For the Turkish Forces, it meant that Louroujina village be taken into the control of Turkish Forces.

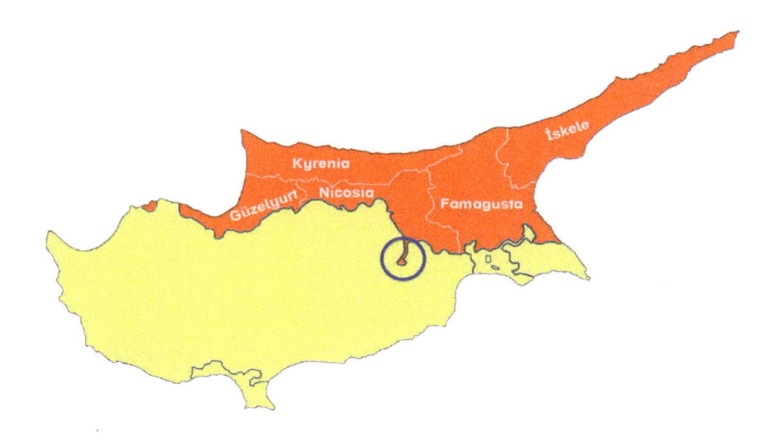

The 17th of August - Asha and Sinta

It was reported that Turkish Forces took eighteen men from Asha village to Sinta village as prisoners of war and they were shot there. The other villagers were deported in two buses and they were shot on the way back from the police headquarters in Nicosia. Total number of missing, presumed dead from the village is given as eighty-three or eighty-four.

The 18th of August - Eptakomi

The village was a mixed village of seventy-five per cent Greek Cypriot and twenty-five per cent Turkish Cypriots. Most of the Greek Cypriot fled fearing for their lives during the Turkish intervention.

It was reported that twelve Greek Cypriot civilians were executed by Turkish Forces with their hands tied behind their backs and their bodies were later found in a mass grave.

The 18th of August – Angolemi

The village was Turkish Cypriot with a population of two hundred and twenty. It was reported that a Turkish Cypriot family of three (father, mother and teenage daughter) and two men were murdered by Greek Cypriot forces (possibly EOKA B).

The 19th of August - Nicosia

Rodger Paul Davies United States American Ambassador to Cyprus, Ms. Antoinette Varnavas, an embassy secretary and a Greek Cypriot national, were killed by sniper fire in the American Embassy, from a nearby building, believed to be by a Greek Cypriot gunman. Afterwards, the United States government "immediately" sent a replacement, Ambassador William R. Crawford Jr., in order to demonstrate that "it was not blaming Greek-Cypriot authorities for the murders."

End of Conflict

By the 19th of August, the major operations of the Cyprus conflict ended and the ceasefire held throughout the island. As the dust settled, the results of the Turkish offensives were apparent. Since the 14th of August, the Turkish Forces had branched out in two directions eastward and westward from their enclaves. It became apparent that it was the Turkish Forces deliberate tactic to allow Greek Cypriot civilians the opportunity to flee before them, thus achieving the "ethnic cleansing" of the area they intended to occupy. The Turkish attacks to the east and west appeared to suggest an effort to form a solid unit in the northern part of the island in accordance with their original plans for establishing an autonomous Turkish State covering about 37 per cent of the island's land.

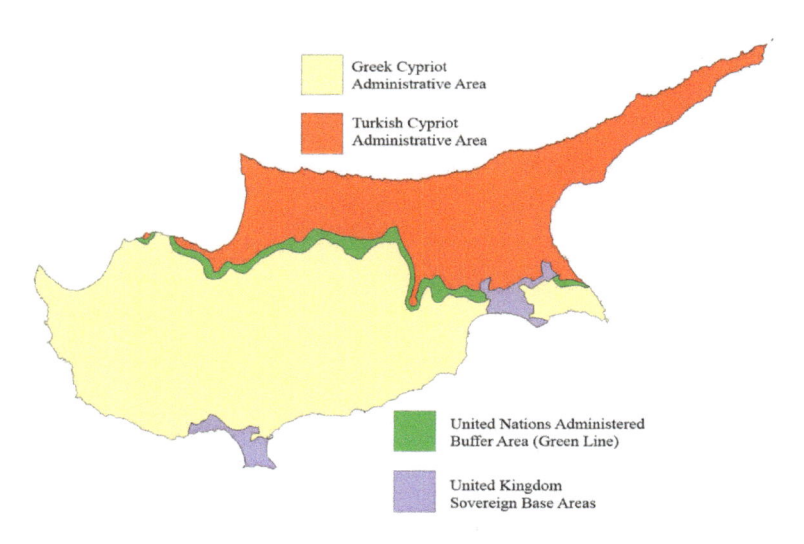

The green line established in 1964 was re-designed. It extends approximately one hundred and eighty kilometres (one hundred and twelve miles) across the island, serving as a physical reminder of the division between the two communities. It was heavily fortified with mines, barbed wire, checkpoints, and military installations, effectively preventing free movement between the divided island. After Attila-II offensive ground to a halt, the two sides consolidated their positions and fortified their respective front lines with trenches, anti-tank ditches, minefields and lines of barbed wire. The Greek Cypriot National Guard made strong efforts to reinstate the units that had suffered severe desertions, and engaged in a major mobilization effort. Deprived of military equipment through attrition and war usage, the Greek Cypriot National Guard relied heavily on re-supply by the Hellenic Navy to meet basic ammunition needs. On the other side, Turkish Forces reinforced their new hold on Northern Cyprus by building major bases, and converting an airfield at Lefkoniko into a functioning military air field with a modest runway. No further major actions occurred after the 19th of August 1974.

Chapter 18
Casualties

United Nations Casualties

Nine United Nations soldiers were killed – three Austrian soldiers, two Danish soldiers, one British soldier, two Canadian soldiers and one Australian civilian policeman. Total nine. Sixty-five were wounded.

Greek Cypriot National Guard Casualties

Estimated Greek Cypriot National Guard soldiers – three hundred and nine were killed, one thousand one hundred and forty-one wounded and nine hundred and nine missing. These figures have not been confirmed.

Greek Regiment (ELDYK) and Greek Army Casualties

Estimated EKDYK and Greek army – eighty-nine were killed, one hundred and forty-eight were wounded and eighty-three missing. These figures have not been confirmed.

Turkish Cypriot Fighters Casualties

Estimated Turkish Cypriot Fighters – seventy were killed and one thousand wounded. These figures have not been confirmed.

Turkish Forces

Estimated Turkish Forces – five hundred and sixty-eight were killed and one thousand two hundred were wounded. These figures have not been confirmed.

Civilian Casualties

As far as I am aware there are no official records of the number of civilians killed. This may be due to the number of missing persons unaccounted for on both sides. Sources suggest different numbers, averaging these sources, the numbers could be in the following regions. Greek Cypriots six thousand and Turkish Cypriots one thousand five hundred plus. The numbers of some Greek Cypriots during the Coup d'état may also have been included in the Turkish intervention figures.

Chapter 19

Evacuations

During the crisis of 1974, the British Sovereign Base Areas. Likewise, HQ UNFICYP and a number of United Nations camps became a safe haven for thousands of Cypriots and foreign nationals fleeing the conflict. It is estimated that upwards of 120,000 people passed through, or sought refuge within these camps at one time or another. These evacuees were evacuated by British Royal Air Force and Royal Navy. In all, it is estimated that 7,929 tourists of 48 different nationalities were evacuated from embattled Cyprus. During the evacuation missions, the British Sovereign Base Area at Dhekelia, Akrotori and UNFICYP played a major part in the organization and execution of that humanitarian operation.

On the 23rd of July 1974 the British Royal Navy ship HMS Hermes and her naval task group, entered Kyrenia harbour war zone and evacuated over one thousand five hundred British and other nationalities from the area.

A number of Greek Cypriots who remained in Kyrenia were held in the Dome Hotel by Turkish Forces. In October 1975 they were taken to Bellapais and transported to the south.

Turkish Cypriots displaced from elsewhere in Cyprus and immigrants from Turkey moved into the vacated Greek Cypriot property. The result is the present ethnic make-up is predominantly Turkish and Turkish-Cypriot in Northern Cyprus.

A total of approximately fifty-one thousand Turkish Cypriots were stranded in the south. Greek Cypriot representatives and the United Nations consented to the transfer of fifty thousand to Northern Cyprus in 1974.

The remaining thousand Turkish Cypriot refugees who refused, or were unable to move north were camped in Episkopi "happy valley" and Paramali forest, British Sovereign Base Area. On the 16th of January 1975 it was unanimously agreed to evacuate them to Northern Cyprus. The following day the transfer commenced and some ten days later it was complete.

There were up to 13,000 dependants of British service personnel located in Cyprus, those not living in married quarters in the Sovereign base areas, were also evacuated during the conflict.

Chapter 20
Missing Persons

As a result of the intervention, over 2000 Greek-Cypriot prisoners of war were taken to Turkey and detained in Turkish prisons. It is alleged some of them were not released and are still missing.

The Committee on Missing Persons (CMP) in Cyprus, which operates under the auspices of the United Nations, is mandated to investigate approximately 1600 cases of Greek Cypriot and Greek missing persons.

The issue of missing persons in Cyprus took a new turn in the summer of 2004 when the United Nations sponsored Committee on Missing Persons (CMP) began returning remains of identified missing individuals to their families.

CMP designed and started to implement its project on the exhumation, identification and return of remains of missing persons. The whole project is being implemented by bi-communal teams of Greek Cypriot and Turkish Cypriot scientists (archaeologists, anthropologists and geneticists) under the overall responsibility of the CMP, to-date 57 individuals have been identified and their remains returned to their families.

The displacement of Greek Cypriots from Northern Cyprus and Turkish Cypriots from Southern Cyprus has left a lasting legacy. Many individuals and families still yearn for resolution, seeking the right to return to their homes and reclaim their properties. The conflict of 1974 left a significant number of missing persons, both Greek and Turkish Cypriots. The issue of missing persons remains a painful reminder of the conflict, with families seeking closure and accountability. Human rights concerns, including minority rights, freedom of movement, and cultural heritage preservation, also persist.

Turkish Cypriot Casualties

Greek Cypriot Missing Persons

Chapter 21
Refugees

It is estimated that between one hundred and forty thousand to one hundred and sixty-five thousand Greek Cypriots and fifty-one thousand Turkish Cypriot refugees were created as a result of the conflict. A massive wave of forced displacement occurred, forcing these displaced communities to vacate their homes and lands as a result. The Turkish Forces paced their offensive to partition the island rather than seek a full annexation. They built their own International Airport, named Ercan International Airport, set up a Turkish Northern Cyprus Government and introduced the Turkish Lira as its currency, it remains so to this day.

The Turkish intervention and forcible division of the island had a profound impact on the demographics, political and territorial changes of the island. As a result, the population of Northern Cyprus became predominantly Turkish and Turkish Cypriot, whereas the south remained predominantly Greek Cypriot.

In 1975, an exchange was carried out whereby Turkish Cypriots in the south could enter the north. Greek Cypriots in the north could enter the south. The exchange was supervised and carried out by United Nations Forces in Cyprus.

Perhaps this is why the majority of Greek Cypriots will forever view the Turkish intervention as an "invasion", whilst Turkish Cypriots who were saved from decades of racial oppression see the operation as a "intervention". From personal discussions in confidence, with a number of Turkish Cypriots in Northern Cyprus in 1977, they still long for their homes in Southern Cyprus, which they were forced to leave and would return if ever the situation became possible.

During the intervention, numerous human rights abuses were carried out by both sides, these included killings, rapes, and looting. Cultural heritage sites, religious institutions, and infrastructure suffered heavy damage or destruction. Greek Orthodox churches, monasteries, and cultural sites were particularly targeted, leading to irreparable loss to the Cyprus' rich cultural heritage.

Chapter 22

Northern Cyprus

Northern Cyprus, the territory occupied by Turkish Forces in 1974, declared its independence in 1983 as the Turkish Republic of Northern Cyprus (TRNC). However, this state is recognized only by Turkey, while the international community considers it an occupied territory of Cyprus. The Turkish military presence in Northern Cyprus continues to this day, with tens of thousands of Turkish troops stationed in the region.

Efforts to find a political solution and reunify the island have been ongoing, with various negotiations and diplomatic initiatives taking place over the years. However, reaching a mutually acceptable agreement has proven to be a complex and challenging task.

For families who lost loved ones in the conflicts, seeking justice and accountability is an ongoing struggle. Investigations into human rights abuses, war crimes, and the disappearance of individuals continue in the pursuit of truth, acknowledgment, and legal recourse. Justice serves as a crucial aspect of the healing process and the quest for closure. Commemoration and Remembrance services should be held in the aftermath of any conflict, to commemorate and remember those who lost their lives. Memorials, monuments, and annual commemorations serve as opportunities for grieving, reflection, and honouring the fallen.

Healing and Reconciliation, the process of healing and reconciliation is deeply intertwined with remembering the fallen. By acknowledging the pain and sacrifices made, communities can foster a sense of empathy, understanding, and collective responsibility. Healing requires the recognition of the shared humanity and interconnectedness of all those who were affected by the conflict.

Lessons for future generations remembering the fallen, offers profound lessons for future generations. It emphasizes the importance of peace, understanding, and dialogue in preventing future conflicts. By learning from the past and appreciating the consequences of violence, younger generations can play a vital role in shaping a more harmonious and peaceful future for the beautiful island of Cyprus.

Chapter 23

European Commission on Human Rights

In 1976 and again in 1983, the European Commission of Human Rights found Turkey guilty of repeated violations of the European Convention of Human Rights. Turkey has been condemned for preventing the return of Greek Cypriot refugees to their properties. The European Commission of Human Rights reports of 1976 and 1983 state the following:

Having found violations of a number of Articles of the Convention, the Commission notes that the acts violating the Convention were exclusively directed against members of one of two communities in Cyprus, namely the Greek Cypriot community. It concludes by eleven votes to three that Turkey has thus failed to secure the rights and freedoms set forth in these Articles without discrimination on the grounds of ethnic origin, race, religion as required by Article 14 of the Convention.

Enclaved Greek Cypriots in the Karpass Peninsula in 1975 were subjected by the Turks to violations of their human rights so that by 2001 when the European Court of Human Rights found Turkey guilty of the violation of 14 articles of the European Convention of Human Rights in its judgement of Cyprus v Turkey (application no. 25781/94), less than 600 still remained. In the same judgement, Turkey was found guilty of violating the rights of the Turkish Cypriots by authorising the trial of civilians by a military court.

The European Commission of Human Rights with 12 votes against 1, accepted evidence from the Republic of Cyprus, concerning the rapes of various Greek-Cypriot women by Turkish soldiers and the torture of many Greek-Cypriot prisoners during the invasion of the island. The high rate of rape reportedly resulted in the temporary permission of abortion in Cyprus by the conservative Cypriot Orthodox Church. Rape was used systematically to "soften" resistance and clear civilian areas through fear. Many of the atrocities were seen as revenge for the atrocities against Turkish Cypriots in 1963–64 and the massacres during the conflicts of 1963/1964. It has been suggested that many of the atrocities were revenge killings, committed by Turkish Cypriot Fighters in military uniform who might have been mistaken for Turkish soldiers. In the Karpass Peninsula, a group of Turkish Cypriots reportedly chose young girls to rape and impregnated teenage girls. There were cases of rapes, which included gang rapes, of teenage girls by Turkish soldiers and Turkish Cypriot men in the peninsula, and one case involved the rape of an old Greek Cypriot man by a Turkish Cypriot. The man was reportedly identified by the victim and two other rapists were also arrested. Raped women were sometimes outcast from society.

Chapter 24

Injustice to Greek Soldiers (ELDYK) Ongoing

Injustice

Not unlike the Irish United Nations soldiers of A Company 35 Infantry Battalion, who served in Jadotville the Congo in 1961, and waited fifty years plus for recognition of their gallant bravery and service from the Irish Government. The Greek Regiment soldiers (ELDYK) who fought bravely and served during the intervention by Turkey of Cyprus, fifty years later they are still being dragged through the Greek courts as they are trying to prove the obvious, namely, that they actually did serve in the war in Cyprus in 1974.

The Greek judicial system has refused to recognise that Greek soldiers of the Hellenic Force in Cyprus (ELDYK) fought in Cyprus during the Turkish intervention in July and August 1974. Despite the fact that eighty-nine were killed, one hundred and forty-eight were wounded, eighty-three missing and their services being recorded in the official documents of the Greek Defence Ministry records.

Surprisingly, the Greek state refused to recognise this reality for decades, until the adoption of a law in 1998 which acknowledged their military service but left a large gap of twenty-four years (from 1974 to 1998) of non-recognition.

These veteran heroes of Cyprus who have appealed to the courts cannot be vindicated, as the Greek Justice system keep referring them either to administrative or civil courts as being the competent bodies to resolve their claim. The Administrative Courts of First Instance and the Court of Appeals award damages for non-pecuniary damage while the Council of State tells them that the civil courts have jurisdiction and to go there again to claim damages.

The even more egregious thing is that the Greek State is demanding these veterans, who served their country by fighting in Cyprus, to return the compensation in case a court had declared a provisionally enforceable decision and had ordered the payment of part of the total compensation it had awarded.

The Lawsuit

In 2003, a lawsuit against the Greek State in the Administrative Court of Athens, claiming that, although they fought against the Turkish Forces in Cyprus by order of authorised officers of the Greek state, Greece was ruled by the Military Junta at the time, the State refused to recognise their military service. The veterans claim that their personality and reputation had been insulted (moral damage) and that this omission of the State had violated the European Convention on Human Rights. In fact, this moral damage was aggravated by "the fact that some Greeks consider them as participants in the coup d'état against the legitimate government of Cyprus." This is untrue the coup d'état was arranged by Greece, the Greek Cypriot National Guard and EOKA B. The veterans claimed 200,000 euro with the legal interest on arrears, as monetary satisfaction for the restoration of their moral damage. The Administrative Court of First Instance of Athens ruled in their favour and awarded each one the amount of 100,000 euro as monetary satisfaction.

The Appeal

The State rescinded to the Administrative Court of Appeal of the First Instance's decision, which in 2011, ruled that this omission of the State "was illegal as contrary to respect for the value of man, which, according to article 2 paragraph 1 of the Constitution, is primary obligation of the State".

The appellants also pointed out that the participants "in these military operations, fulfilling their supreme obligation as Greek citizens, expected that their offer would be recognized at least by the official State and would not be ignored or silenced" and ratified the amount as compensation of 100,000 euro awarded to them.

Again, the State filed an appeal with the Court of Appeals against the appellate decision. Ten years after the State's appeal, the State Councillors ruled that the reasonable time in which they could claim their claims in the administrative courts had expired and that "the civil courts now have jurisdiction".

In other words, fifty years after the intervention in Cyprus, twenty four years after the partial recognition by the Greek state of their military service in Cyprus, twenty one years after the filing of the lawsuit in the Court of First Instance, and ten years after the stay of the appeal in the State Counsellors against the Court of Appeal, the State Counsellors are now saying to those who fought in Cyprus against the invader to start from scratch in the civil courts (Court of First Instance). The red tape all over again.

The absurdity

As if all this were not enough, the State requested the Council of State to return the amount of compensation that had probably been temporarily awarded to them. The State Council rejected the request, as it did not appear that any part of the compensation had been paid out to the veterans. They are still awaiting recognition, justice and compensation.

Chapter 25
Economic Effects of Partition

Republic of Cyprus

The economic achievements of Cyprus during the preceding decades since have been significant, bearing in mind the severe economic and social dislocation created by the Turkish intervention of 1974 and the continuing occupation of the northern part of the island by Turkey. The Turkish intervention inflicted a serious blow to the Cyprus economy in the agriculture, mining and quarrying. 70% of the island's wealth-producing resources were lost, the tourist industry lost 65% of its hotels and tourist accommodation, the industrial sector lost 46%, and mining and quarrying lost 56% of production. The loss of the port of Famagusta, which handled 83% of the general cargo, and the closure of Nicosia International Airport, in the buffer zone, were additional setbacks.

The success of Cyprus in the economic sphere has been attributed, inter alia, to the adoption of a market-oriented economic system, the pursuance of sound macroeconomic policies by the government as well as the existence of a dynamic and flexible entrepreneurship and a highly educated labour force. Moreover, the economy benefited from the close cooperation between the public and private sectors.

In the past 50 years, the economy has shifted from agriculture to light manufacturing and services. The services sector, including tourism, contributes almost 80% to GDP and employs more than 70% of the labour force. Industry and construction account for approximately one-fifth of GDP and labour, while agriculture is responsible for 2.1% of GDP and 8.5% of the labour force.

Through vigorous efforts, real growth was resumed in the area that remained under the control of the government of the Republic of Cyprus and between 1975 and 1983 the annual rate of growth was estimated to average over 10%. Since 1983 the economy of the Greek Cypriot sector has flourished, unemployment and inflation have remained relatively low. Tourism has provided the main leverage of economic growth, and many areas have undergone technological upgrading. In the 1990s the Greek Cypriot sector increasingly transformed itself into a centre of international transit trade, merchant shipping, banking, and related services. The Republic's Greek Cypriot run government established special tariff arrangements with the European Union and foreign organization, whose member countries account for about half of the island's imports. The Greek Cypriot sector joined the European Union in 2004 and adopted the euro as its official currency in 2008.

In the years following the dissolution of the Soviet Union it gained great popularity as a portal for investment from the West into Russia and Eastern Europe, becoming for companies of that origin the most common tax haven. More recently, there have been increasing investment flows from the west through Cyprus into Asia, particularly China and India, South America and the Middle East. In addition, businesses from outside the European Union use Cyprus as their entry-point for investment into Europe. Following the 2022 Russian invasion of Ukraine, Cyprus businesses and individuals have come under scrutiny and criticism for allowing European Union and United States sanctions to be breached with belated attempts to stop them or bring the culprits to justice. A number of professional law and accounting firms have been identified as helping Russian Oligarchs evade sanctions.

Turkish Republic of Northern Cyprus

The economy is dominated by the services sector (69% of GDP in 2007), which includes the public sector, trade, tourism and education. Industry (light manufacturing) contributes 22% of GDP and agriculture 9%. Northern Cyprus's economy operates on a free-market basis, with a significant portion of administration costs funded by Turkey. The Turkish Republic of Northern Cyprus uses the Turkish lira as its currency, which links its economic situation to the economy of Turkey. Because of its international status and the embargo on its ports, the Turkish Republic of Northern Cyprus is heavily dependent on Turkish military and economic support from Turkey. All their exports and imports have to take place via Turkey, unless they are produced locally, from materials sourced in the area (or imported via one of the island's recognised ports) when they may be exported via one of the legal ports. Although their economy has developed in recent years, it is still dependent on monetary transfers from the Turkish government. Under a July 2006 agreement, Ankara shall provide Northern Cyprus with an economic aid in the amount of $1.3 billion over three years (2006–2008). This is a continuation of ongoing policy under which the Turkish government allocates around $400 million annually from its budget to help raise the living standards of the Turkish Cypriots and Turkish Nationalists.

The tourism sector of Northern Cyprus has seen high levels of constant growth. 1.23 million tourists visited Northern Cyprus in 2018, 920,000 of these being from Turkey. The number of tourists is increasing yearly. The growth was further increased by the arrival of North European home buyers, investing in holiday villas. Over 10,000 British people, including expatriates purchased holiday villas to live in permanently, or to visit during the summer months. This generated over $1 Billion.

Trade between the two areas ceased in 1974, and the two economies have remained independent. However, the Republic of Cyprus continues to supply the Turkish Republic of Northern Cyprus with electricity. The

Turkish Republic of Northern Cyprus still processes the sewage system of the Greek Cypriot area of Nicosia.

The continuing Cyprus problem adversely affects the economic development of the Turkish Republic of Northern Cyprus. The Republic of Cyprus, as the internationally recognised authority, has declared airports and ports in the area not under its effective control, closed. All United Nations and European Union member countries accept the closure of those ports and airports according to the declaration of the Republic of Cyprus. The Turkish community argues that the Republic of Cyprus has used its international standing to handicap economic relations between them and the rest of the world. The current situation in Cyprus may hamper Turkey if they make application to join European Union.

Chapter 26
Conclusion

Divided territories create their own ugly landmarks. In Nicosia, now holder of the unenviable distinction of being the world's last divided capital city, the scars of the conflict are evident. Likewise, across the entire green line. They come in the form of a United Nations patrolled green line area, a scar that runs east to west across the city, the island and in the dereliction that surrounds it. Roads end at barrels and barbed wire, buildings stand bullet-pocked and empty, gun ports, sandbags and sentry posts slowly decay.

For fifty years these dismal sights have provided the motif to a conflict frozen in time, the most potent symbol of a one hundred and twelve-mile ceasefire line that has kept Cyprus's estranged Christian Orthodox Greek Cypriots and Muslim Turkish Cypriot communities apart.

Since the Republic of Cyprus is a member of European Union, it has taken an interest in the situation in Cyprus in conjunction with United Nations. The European Union would like to resolve the issue and stabilize relations with Turkey. But the Turkish Cypriots want them out of the talks completely, so it can deal purely with the Greek Cypriot government.

The Turkish Republic of Northern Cyprus claim the European Union is missing the point with cycles of diplomacy focused on a federal unification of Cyprus and has to accept a two-state solution on the divided island. They also claim the European Union are continually doing the same thing, nothing is changing. Federal settlement plans have been discussed for fifty years, nothing has been achieved. The United Nations know this, European

Union know this, and they come up every six months with the same thing, that you should sit at the table to discuss the Cyprus settlement on a federal basis. Since Cyprus is already a European Union member, the bloc rallies behind the internationally recognized Greek Cypriot government. Some member states, like Germany, have attempted to break the gridlock and broker deals, Greek Cypriots have no incentive to back down from their maximalist demands. That limits Turkey and Turkish Cypriots' manoeuvring room, to grid locking the process.

The Republic of Cyprus shows no inclination to agree to the recognition of the Turkish Republic of Northern Cyprus. In general, Greek Cypriots treat the Republic of Cyprus' sovereignty over the entire island of Cyprus as indisputable. They point to United Nations Security Council resolutions referencing a single government for the island, and to Protocol 10 of Cyprus' accession act to the European Union, which designates the northern part of Cyprus as a Republic of Cyprus territory, albeit one "on which the government cannot exercise control". They argue that the north's growing reliance on Ankara further undercuts its insistence on being treated as an independent sovereign entity at the negotiating table. Greek Cypriots want all the properties in the area of Varosha/Maraş returned to the Greek Cypriot persons and businesses who legally own them, and the territory transferred to UN administration, as per UN Security Council Resolutions 550 and 789 and all Greek Cypriot properties in the Turkish Republic of Northern Cyprus.

Property rights were incorporated in the 1948 United Nations Universal Declaration of Human Rights (article 17), it is protected by the European Convention (article 1, Protocol I), and by the Charter of Fundamental Rights of the European Union (article 17). In addition to their legal and economic aspects, property rights in Cyprus are also an important indicator of heritage and identity.

After more than five decades of failed talks it is hard to see a clear way forward to the reunification of Cyprus, or even to talks about reunification. Tensions threaten to deepen rifts in the eastern Mediterranean and sour Turkish –European Union relations, while aggravating old disagreements and creating new ones between Ankara and its NATO allies. Among other things, the impasse between Cyprus' two main communities underline the limits of pressure tactics for both sides. Decades of isolation and economic pressure have led Turkish Cypriots to closer ties with Ankara, non-acceptance of Greek Cypriot terms. Turkish military posturing and turn away from negotiations, have not led the Republic of Cyprus to recognise the Turkish Cypriot entity as sovereign and equal. There is some similarity with the Northern Ireland problem where some want union with the Republic of Ireland and others want to maintain union with Great Britain in a divided island. In addition to the two communities in Northern Ireland, the governments of Great Britain and of the Republic of Ireland have a stake in resolving the problem.

In Cyprus, the governments of Turkey and of Greece are similarly involved as stakeholders. In the case of Cyprus, the United Nations specifically and the international community generally plus the European Union has found negotiations challenging because of lack of willingness by the two-sides to compromise. In assessing the effectiveness of United Nations peace-keeping, it can only be effective in situations when "all parties to a conflict sought to end it and needed the good offices of a neutral force to reinforce mutual trust or verify their fulfilment of obligations". Due to lack of progress towards a negotiated solution, effectively, the United Nations peace-keepers have merely controlled a buffer zone between the Greek Cypriot and Turkish controlled areas of the island for fifty years. Unwillingness by both sides to cooperate with the United Nations in negotiating a peaceful and viable solution has handicapped the negotiations process. Recognizing that civil society in Cyprus requires nurturing so that members of the two communities can begin to establish better understanding, replacing hostility with friendship, many Non-Governmental Organizations (NGOs) are active on the island. Initiatives aim to create personal links and ties between the two communities. By creating opportunities for people to meet across the communitarian divide, reconciliation becomes a more likely prospect. The Non-Government Organisations (NGOs) are hoping to stimulate a thirst for reconciliation and an equitable solution to inform a groundswell of popular support for a sustainable solution. They must reach out their hands in friendship to the other side and give the people of both communities a reason to believe in sincerity and goodwill. A willingness to listen to the pain and suffering that both sides have experienced. Quit the rhetoric of blame, and accept responsibility for their own community's contribution, both from the past and now, to the Cyprus problem. Give up the idea of using violence, force and that each side are enemies, as a means to settle problems. View as legitimate the needs and concerns of the other community. The path to peace is through rough and unexplored territory, full of monsters that appear ready to swallow all of us at any moment in time. Peace can be made between both communities; it will take time, effort, sweat, tears, co-operation and sacrifices. This may seem impossible after fifty years' negotiations with stalemate, but both communities can eventually come to some solution to the Cyprus problem.

With no comprehensive deal in reach for the time being, the parties should try a more conciliatory approach, looking to cooperate for mutual benefit, for example in support of trade and travel, and to take other small steps together. To create an atmosphere conducive to such steps, Greek Cypriots will probably need to be assured that a future political settlement will return to them the long fenced-off areas of Varosha/Maraş. It is time for them to change course for the benefit of their own communities, as well as for peace and security in the eastern Mediterranean.

End

Abbreviations

AUSCON	Austrian Contingent
AUSTCIVPOL	Australian Civil Police
BRITCON	British Contingent
CANCON	Canadian Contingent
ELDYK	Greek Regiment
EMAK	National Front of Cyprus
EOKA	National Organisation of Cypriot Fighters
ENOSIS	Union with Greece
FINCON	Finnish Contingent
IRCON	Irish Contingent
KTKA	Turkish Regiment
NATO	North Atlantic Treaty Organisation
NGO	Non-Governmental Organisations
RAF	Royal Air Force
RCT	Royal Corps of Transport
SBA	Sovereign Base Area
SWEDCON	Swedish Contingent
TNT	Turkish Cypriot Fighters
UNFICYP	United Nations Forces in Cyprus

Acknowledgements

Irish Defence Forces - Information from website

Major Vincent McEllin Royal Irish Guards - Extract from his story. Brigadier General Jimmy Flynn DSM (RIP)

Robert Cantwell – Cover design, page text and photo editing

Michael Feeney OBE – General advice

Moira Gammon – Proof reading

Des Howe - Some photographs

Mark Godfrey – Western People

Mid-West Radio

To my comrades in Defence Forces for the excellent work they carry out at home and on United Nations Missions worldwide, may you continue the good work into the future. To my friends in the Irish United Nations Veterans Association, Organisation of National Ex-Service Personnel, Association of Retired Commissioned Officers and to all other Veteran's Associations, I express my heartfelt gratitude for the excellent services you carry out for the welfare of all our Veterans and the Commemoration Services for our fallen heroes. To members of the Gardaí Siochana who served and are still serving on United Nations missions worldwide.

If I have left anyone out, it is not intentional and I apologise.

Supplementary

Ireland and United Nations
- Roll of Honour
- Current UN Missions
- Past Missions
- Irish United Nations Veterans Association
- Association of Retired Commissioned Officers
- Other Veteran associations
- General

Roll of Honour

Listed below are the names of Irish Soldiers who gave their lives for the cause of peace on United Nations Missions.

Remember Them

Congo (ONUC)

Ser	No.	Rank	Name	O/Seas Unit	Home Unit	Date Deceased
1	80322	CS	Felix Grant DSM	33 Inf Bn	12 Inf Bn	3/10/1960
2	0.4350	Col	Justin MacCarthy	HQ ONUC	HQ 4 W Bde	27/10/1960
3	0.7500	Lt	Kevin Gleeson	33 Inf Bn	2 Fd Engr Coy	08/11/1960
4	804359	Sgt	Hugh F Gaynor	33 Inf Bn	2 Mot Sqn	08/11/1960
5	804234	Cpl	Liam Dougan	33 Inf Bn	5 Inf Bn	08/11/1960
6	809239	Cpl	Peter Kelly	33 Inf Bn	5 Inf Bn	08/11/1960
7	804536	Pte	Matthew Farrell	33 Inf Bn	2 Hosp Coy	08/11/1960
8	808548	Tpr	Thomas Fennell	33 Inf Bn	2 Mot Sqn	08/11/1960
9	806115	Tpr	Anthony Browne MMG	33 Inf Bn	2 Mot Sqn	08/11/1960
10	802900	Pte	Michael McGuinn	33 Inf Bn	2 Fd Engr Coy	08/11/1960
11	810242	Pte	Gerard Killeen	33 Inf Bn	CTD (E)	08/11/1960
12	806785	Pte	Patrick H Davis	33 Inf Bn	2 Fd Engr Coy	10/11/1960
13	806855	Cpl	Liam Kelly	33 Inf Bn	3 Inf Bn	24/12/1960
14	422602	Cpl	Luke Kelly	HQ ONUC	Dep MPC	30/08/1961
15	808594	Tpr	Edward Gaffney	35 Inf Bn	1 Armd Car Sqn	13/09/1961
16	810552	Tpr	Patrick Mullins	35 Inf Bn	1 Mot Sqn	15/09/1961
17	806566	Cpl	Michael Nolan	35 Inf Bn	1 Tk Sqn	15/091961
18	810568	Cpl	Michael Fallon	36 Inf Bn	5 Inf Bn	08/12/1961
19	87410	Sgt	Patrick Mulcahy DSM	36 Inf Bn	6 Fd Arty Regt	16/12/1961
20	0.7776	Lt	Patrick A Riordan DSM	36 Inf Bn	6 Fd Arty Regt	16/12/1961
21	812054	Pte	Andrew Wickham	36 Inf Bn	2 Inf Bn	16/12/1961

22	87602	Cpl	John Geoghegan	36 Inf Bn	15 Inf Bn	28/12/1961
23	811849	Cpl	John Power	36 Inf Bn	CTD (E)	07/03/1962
24	0.6769	Capt	Ronald L McCann	HQ ONUC	CTD (W)	09/05/1962
25	80453	Cpl	John McGrath	38 Inf Bn	4 Hosp Coy	21/03/1963
26	0.6536	Comdt	Thomas McMahon	HQ ONUC	HQ W Comd	28/09/1963

Cyprus (UNFICYP)

27	87770	CS	Wallace J MacAuley	41 Inf Bn	Dep MPC	22/02/1965
28	99093	Sgt	John Hamill	4 Inf Gp	Dep Cav	7/04/1965
29	815345	Cpl	William Hetherington	4 Inf Gp	CTD (E)	19/07/1965
30	405923	CS	James Ryan	6 Inf Gp	5 Inf Bn	04/10/1966
31	0.7778	Capt	Christopher McNamara	9 Inf Gp	2 Grn S&T Coy	16/01/1968
32	808052	Cpl	James Fagan	10 Inf Gp	2 Mot Sqn	10/06/1968
33	0.8006	Lt	Ronald B Byrne	11 Inf Gp	4 Inf Bn	28/10/1968
34	817553	Tpr	Michael Kennedy	12 Inf Gp	1 Armd Car Sqn	01/07/1969
35	818694	Pte	Brendan Cummins	20 Inf Gp	2 Inf Bn	11/06/1971

Middle East (UNTSO)

| 36 | 0.6374 | Comdt | Thomas P Wickham | UNTSO | HQ C Comd | 07/06/1967 |
| 37 | 0.8181 | Comdt | Michael Nestor | UNTSO | Mil Col | 25/09/1982 |

Lebanon (UNIFIL)

38	836707	Pte	Gerard Moon	43 Inf Bn	4 Inf Bn	25/08/1978
39	829745	Cpl	Thomas Reynolds	44 Inf Bn	2 Grn S&T Coy	24/12/1978
40	839148	Pte	Philip Grogan	UNIFIL HQ	28 Inf Bn	10/07/1979
41	830497	Pte	Stephen Griffin	46 Inf Bn	1 Fd Engr Coy	16/04/1980
42	830818	Pte	Thomas Barrett	46 Inf Bn	4 Inf Bn	18/04/1980
43	828468	Pte	Derek Smallhorne	46 Inf Bn	5 Inf Bn	18/08/1980
44	813376	Sgt	Edward Yates	47 Inf Bn	2 Cav Sqn	31/05/1980
45	841137	Cpl	Vincent Duffy	47 Inf Bn	6 Fd Sig Coy	18/10/1980
46	838459	Pte	John Marshall	48 Inf Bn	6 Fd S&T Coy	17/12/1980

47	815518	CS	James Martin	UNIFIL HQ	4 Grn MP Coy	10/02/1981
48	841576	Pte	Caoimhín Seoighe	48 Inf Bn	1 Cn Cois	27/04/1981
49	840638	Pte	Hugh Doherty	49 Inf Bn	28 Inf Bn	27/04/1981
50	837731	Pte	Niall Byrne	49 Inf Bn	6 Inf Bn	22/06/1981
51	826828	Pte	Gerard Hodges	50 Inf Bn	CTD (S)	20/03/1982
52	843152	Pte	Peter Burke	52 Inf Bn	5 Inf Bn	27/10/1982
53	841689	Cpl	Gregory Morrow	52 Inf Bn	2 Inf Bn	27/10/1982
54	843886	Pte	Thomas Murphy	52 Inf Bn	2 Inf Bn	27/10/1982
55	843587	Cpl	George Murray	55 Inf Bn	2 Grn MP Coy	09/10/1984
56	844963	Tpr	Paul Fogarty	59 Inf Bn	1 Tk Sqn	20/07/1986
57	0.9222	Lt	Aengus Murphy	59 Inf Bn	AAS	21/08/1986
58	850413	Pte	William O'Brien	60 Inf Bn	6 Inf Bn	06/12/1986
59	848100	Cpl	Dermot McLoughlin	60 Inf Bn	28 Inf Bn	10/01/987
60	830670	Sgt Maj	John Fitzgerald	UNIFIL HQ	1 Fd Arty Regt	24/02/1987
61	828854	Cpl	George Bolger	61 Inf Bn	12 Inf Bn	29/08/1987
62	851307	Gnr	Paul Cullen	62 Inf Bn	2 Fd Arty Regt	17/03/1988
63	848545	Pte	Patrick Wright	63 Inf Bn	27 Inf Bn	21/08/1988
64	851270	Pte	Michael McNeela	64 Inf Bn	27 Inf Bn	24/02/1989
65	844701	Cpl	Fintan Heneghan	64 Inf Bn	1 Cn Cois	21/03/1989
66	844789	Pte	Thomas Walsh	64 Inf Bn	28 Inf Bn	21/03/1989
67	843237	Pte	Mannix Armstrong	64 Inf Bn	28 Inf Bn	21/03/1989
68	837612	Sgt	Charles Forrester	65 Inf Bn	2 Fd Arty Regt	21/05/1989
69	0.8527	Comdt	Michael O'Hanlon	66 Inf Bn	HQ C Comd	21/11/1989
70	848020	Cpl	Michael McCarthy	70 Inf Bn	4 Inf Bn	15/11/1991
71	843715	Cpl	Peter Ward	71 Inf Bn	6 Inf Bn	29/09/1992
72	842626	Cpl	Martin Tynan	72 Inf Bn	Dep MPC	13/12/1992
73	830851	CQMS	Declan Stokes	28 Ir Comp	Mil Col	14/06/1993
74	848554	Armn	Stephen O'Connor	73 Inf Bn	Air Corps	03/10/993
75	846385	Sgt	John Lynch	36 Ir Comp	HQ C Comd	06/08/1997
76	851719	Pte	Michael Dowling	83 Inf Bn	30 Inf Bn	16/09/1998
77	856952	Pte	Kevin Barrett	84 Inf Bn	28 Inf Bn	18/08/1999
78	856301	Pte	William Kedian	85 Inf Bn	1 Cois Cn	31/05/1999
79	854526	Tpr	Jonathan Campbell	85 Inf Bn	4 Cav Sqn	05/09/1999

80	857259	Pte	Declan Deere	86 Inf Bn	3 Inf Bn	14/02/2000
81	857331	Pte	Brendan Fitzpatrick	86 Inf Bn	3 Inf Bn	14/02/2000
82	857266	Pte	Matthew Lawlor	86 Inf Bn	3 Inf Bn	14/02/2000
83	857271	Pte	Jonathan Murphy	86 Inf Bn	3 Inf Bn	14/02/2000
84	869674	Pte	Seán Rooney	121 Inf Bn	27 Inf Bn	14/12/2022

East Timor (UNTAET)

| 85 | 858175 | Pte | Peadar Ó Flaithearta | 8 IRCON | 1 Cn Cois | 15/04/2002 |

Liberia (UNMIL)

| 86 | 852480 | Sgt | Derek Mooney | 90 Inf Bn | ARW | 27/11/2003 |

EU/Nordic Battle Group

| 87 | 0.8862 | Lt Col | Paul Delaney | EU/NBG HQ | 2 Inf Bn (Gen List) | 23/07/2007 |

EU Military Staff, Brussels

| 88 | 0.9611 | Lt Col | John 'Jack' Griffin | EUMS | J2 DFHQ | 31/10/2015 |

They shall not hear the bittern cry
In the wild sky where they are lain
Nor voices of the sweeter birds
Above the wailing of the rain
Nor shall they know when loud March blows
Thro' slanting snows her fanfare shrill
Blowing to flame the golden cup
Of many an upset daffodil
And when the dark cow leaves the moor
And pastures poor with greedy weeds
Perhaps they'll her low at morn
Lifting her horn in pleasant meads
"Then we shall remember their heroic deeds"

By Francis Ledwidge

Irish Defence Forces

Irish Defence Forces – Current UN Missions

Middle East

Location	Mission	Dates
Syria/ Jordan/ Lebanon/ Israel	UNTSO	December 1958 to date
Lebanon	UNIFIL	May 1978 to date
Golan Heights	UNDOF	September 2013 to date

Irish Defence Forces - Past UN Missions

European Missions

Location	Mission	Dates
Cyprus	UNFICYP	March 1964 - May 2005
Yugoslavia	UNHCR (Y)	December 1992 - March 1993
Serbia and Croatia	UNPROFOR	January 1992 - January 1996
Federal Republic of Yugoslavia	UNMOP	February 1996 - December 1999
Former Yugoslavia	UNTAES	February 1996 - January 1998
Kosovo	UNMIK	August 1999 - 21 Oct 2010

Middle East

Location	Mission	Dates
Lebanon	UNOGIL	June 1958 - December 1958
Suez Canal/Golan Heights	UNEF II	October 1973 - September 1974
Golan Heights	UNDOF	June 1977 - August 1988
Iran	UNIT	June 1984 - July 1988
Lebanon	UNRWA	February 1988 - June 1992

Iran/Iraq	UNIIMOG	August 1988 - March 1991
Iraq/Kuwait	UNIKOM	April 1991 - March 2002
Iraq	UNSCOM	September 1996 - March 2003

African Missions

Location	Mission	Dates
Congo	UNOC	July 1960 - June 1964
Namibia	UNTAG	March 1989 - April 1990
Angola	UNAVEM II	July 1991 - September 1993
Somalia	UNOSOM II	August 1993 - January 1995
Ethiopia &Eritrea	UNMEE	November 2001 - June 2003
Cote d'Ivoire	MINUCI	2003 - 2004
Liberia	UNMIL	November 2003 - May 2007
Chad	MINURCAT	March 2009 - December 2010
Cote d'Ivoire	UNOCI	April 2004 - 2016
Western Sahara	MINURSO	September 1991 - July 2021
Congo	MONUSCO	June 2001 - August 2022
Mali	MINUSMA	September 2019 - Sept 2022

Central American Missions

Location	Mission	Dates
Central America	ONUCA	December 1989 - January 1999
El Salvador	ONUSAL	January 1992 - May 1994
Haiti	UNMIH	September 1994 - March 1996

Asian Missions

Location	Mission	Dates
Indonesia	UNTEA	August 1962 - October 1962
India/Pakistan	UNIPOM	September 1965 - March 1966
Afghanistan	UNGOMAP	April 1988 - March 1990
Cambodia	UNAMIC/ UNTAC	November 1991 - November 1993
East Timor	UNAMET/ UNTAET	July 1999 - May 2002

Jim Casey

Irish Veteran Associations

Irish Hero's – Veterans Day Collins Barracks Dublin

Irish United Nations Veterans Association

The Irish United Nations Veterans Association (IUNVA) was formed at a meeting 1989 and approved by the then Minister of Defence. The Association is non-denominational, non-political and non-sectarian. IUNVA is Charity Registered Association. Membership is available to any Irish resident who has successfully completed a tour of duty with a UN Force or Organisation, whether he or she is serving or retired. The Association is organised with a National Executive HQ and a number of "Posts" throughout the country.

The Main Objective of the Association is to ensure that the memory of those who gave their lives in the cause of peace on United Nations service is not forgotten. To remember deceased non-members who served in Defence Forces and Gardaí.

Membership is offered to anyone resident in Ireland not necessarily Irish or an Irish citizen living abroad and ex members of the Defence Forces, Foreign Armies and Gardaí or Civilians who have served at least 90 days' service or successfully completed a tour of duty on a UN mission.

For more information:

Visit the IUNVA Website
www.iunva.ie

Óglaigh Náisiúnta na hÉireann

Organisation of National Ex-Service Personnel

Óglaigh Náisiúnta na hÉireann (Organisation of National Ex-Service Personnel - ONE) is a registered charity for veterans of the Defence Forces. It was established on 10th of March 1951, incorporated as charitable company limited by guarantee in 2000, and has approximately 1,500 members.

The work of ONE can be summarised in four words – Support, Comradeship, Advocacy, & Remembrance. The primary objective of ONE is to Support the needs of Irish veterans by the provision of accommodation to homeless and other veterans in need of such domestic accommodation in its Veterans' Hostels, and the provision of other advice and support to veterans through its nationwide network of Branches and Veterans' Support Centres.

ONE has three hostels for homeless veterans in Dublin, Donegal and Westmeath, with a further facility under development in Cobh, Co. Cork. In addition, ONE has 36 Branches across the country and a nationwide network of 15 Veteran Support Centres. ONE provides just under 18,000 bed nights to veterans every year in our hostels, with 95% of the veterans we help moving on to permanent housing. The hostels have 49 single rooms and that will increase to 60 following the development of the Cobh hostel and a further hostel in the Munster area.

A recent awareness campaign about the work of ONE can be found on **sleepingflags.ie** .

For more information:

Visit the O.N.E website
www.one-veterans.org

Association of Retired Commissioned Officers

ARCO was founded in 1993 and its purpose is to represent retired officers of the Permanent Defence Force of Ireland. The association has some 800 members. Its main focus has always been on pension issues and the website provides members with information on this, along with details on a broad range of other issues and events.

For more information:

Visit the ARCO Website
www.arcoireland.com

Other Veteran Associations

There are a number of other associations/organisations of ex-Irish Defence Forces Personnel established throughout the country. We have the Royal British Legion Ireland and a number of their members have set up their own Regiments/Battalions associations/organisations. We also have the French Foreign Legion Veterans Association of Ireland.

As veterans we endeavour to work closely together for the welfare of all veterans. We participate in each other's Commemorations and events plus Government run Ceremonies.

General

The 1960's

Many of my comrades from the 1960's have passed away; they will remain in my memory until I join them. One could trust them and the ones still alive to-day with their lives, their loyalty and comradeship was beyond reproach. Our military training was of the highest standard possible.

Unfortunately, our kit, equipment and weaponry were not up to the standard of a modern army. This was soon to change with our deployment to United Nations Missions. On the initial missions we had not the suitable kit, equipment and weaponry for such missions, this was not required, so we adapted a different approach. We approached all incidents in a non-aggressive, impartial and a humanitarian manner, but strict to the point when necessary and never taking sides. Of course, "the gift of the Irish Brogue" had an overpowering satisfactory result in most cases. Our unusual methods of approach soon spread to the warring factions and most of them showed the highest regard and respect to us.

The deployment to United Nations Missions opened a new world to the Irish Defence Forces. Ninety-nine per cent of us were never on an aeroplane before, or seen a foreign individual, except perhaps working in a hospital. For the first time we could serve in foreign countries, meet and communicate with their citizens and experience their customs. This was an education in itself.

From working with the other United Nations Contingents, we gained a vast amount of military experience in different military fields and operational procedures. We participated in all the United Nations sporting events, normally winning the shooting competitions, soccer, basketball and excelled at the other events.

In Lebanon at the final of a soccer match between Irish Batt and Ghan Batt, at the start the Ghanaians had a witchdoctor perform his magic tactics on the Irish goal. Out of nowhere at the Ghanaian goal appeared St. Patrick himself, (the late John D (RIP) dressed in full attire and likewise he danced and copied the witchdoctor's tactics. The Ghanaian players and supporters went berserk; they could not believe what they were witnessing. St. Patrick's tactics worked we won three goals to one.

Not only did we make contact with other United Nations Contingents, in Cyprus we made some good relationships with the British Forces stationed in the Sovereign Base Areas. In 1969, the 12th Infantry Group fielded a hurling team against the Irish Guards. This is a brief reduced extract of a piece written by Captain Vincent McEllin, Assistant Regimental Adjutant Irish Guards. He is originally from Manulla, Castlebar, Co. Mayo. It's from a section written by him, in the book Remembering Mayo's Fallen Heroes, by Michael Feeney OBE.

"One event I will always remember took place in Cyprus in 1969, when our Irish Guards played a hurling match against the Irish Contingent (UNFICYP). The match took place in the cool evening watched by Europeans, locals and a battery of cameras. In attendance were, Brig. Davies-Scourfield, Dhekelia Area Commander, Lt. Gen. Sir Basil Eugester, the Regiment Lieutenant Colonel, Irish Guards, Lt. Col. Hassey and Comdt. Quinn Irish Army and Lt. Col. Head, CO 1st Battalion Irish Guards.

The Irish (UNFICYP) and the 1st Battalion Irish Guards pipe bands led the teams onto the converted cricket pitch. The Irish Army (UNFICYP) team made all the play in the first half, leading by 3 goals and 1 point to 3 points. The second half saw a resurgence of the Irish Guards and the melee around the Irish goal post was a memorial sight which brought a goal to the Irish Guards. Midway through the second half the referee noticed 16 players on the Irish Guards team and gave the extra man his marching orders, amidst resounding laughter from the spectators. The Irish (UNFICYP) team finally recovered scoring a spate of points making the final score Irish (UNFICYP) 3 goals and 8 points to 1 goal and 3 points Irish Guards.

After the presentation of plaques and handshakes all availed of a buffet in Elizabeth Barracks. That night, and the following morning, the gatherings of the O' and Macs' took place in various messes and NAFFI, where Irish Guardsmen and Irish (UNFICYP) soldiers, not to mention Arthur Guinness, shook hands and sang to the accompaniment of the combined 40 strong pipe bands. A besieged Greek barman did his best to cope and swore to Aphrodite that never in his 20 years with NAFFI service had seen such a sight.

During my service I have been privileged to serve alongside the Irish Army in other parts of the world but the memory of that event in Cyprus will stay with me."

The above is true, to the best of my knowledge, as I was a spectator at the match and took part in the celebrations afterwards. The story doesn't end here. On a Friday evening in July 2018, after a meeting at Irish United Nations Veterans Association I was travelling from Dublin to Mayo on the train. This huge gentleman wearing a jeans and t-shirt sat opposite me. He said good afternoon in a strong American accent. I asked where he came from in America, he replied he was Irish and originally from Tullamore, and said he was home after fifty-five years for his mother's funeral two days ago.

He then noticed the badge on my blazer and asked if it was a UN badge, I replied it was a UN Veterans badge. He asked was I ever in Cyprus, stating he served there with the Irish Rangers, but left and went to America in 1970. I said I served a number of times in Cyprus, I was astonished when he then said I played on the Irish Guards hurling team against the 12th Infantry Group in 1969. I replied I was a spectator at the game, this was such a coincidence, it's unbelievable. We got so deep in conversation he forgot to get off at Tullamore and went as far as Athlone.

There were many more sporting, other events and stories to tell, but far too many to mention. It is my belief that the initial deployments on United Nations Service by the Irish Soldiers in the 1960's, kick-started the development of the Irish Defence Forces to what it is to-day. One of the most professional proficient armies in the world, with the most modern up to date equipment, weapons and armoury.

I left the army in 1986, as a member of the Irish United Nations Veterans Association and the Irish Parachute Club I am still in contact with current serving members who keep me up to date on new developments and we have many a discussion on past times.

The End

Milton Keynes UK
Ingram Content Group UK Ltd.
UKHW050736090824
446759UK00020B/232